Old Burial Grounds
of New Jersey

Old Burial Grounds of New Jersey

A Guide

Janice Kohl Sarapin

RUTGERS UNIVERSITY PRESS
New Brunswick, New Jersey

Library of Congress Cataloging-in-Publication Data

Sarapin, Janice Kohl.
    Old burial grounds of New Jersey : a guide / by Janice Kohl
Sarapin.
      p.   cm.
    Includes bibliographical references and index.
    ISBN 0-8135-2110-6 (cloth) — ISBN 0-8135-2111-4 (pbk.)
    1. New Jersey—Guidebooks. 2. Cemeteries—New Jersey—Guidebooks.
3. New Jersey—Genealogy—Handbooks, manuals, etc.   I. Title.
F132.S27   1994
917.4904'43—dc20   94-14635
                                             CIP

British Cataloging-in-Publication information available

Contents

Part Two
A Guide to Notable New Jersey Burial Grounds

Preface

OLD BURIAL grounds fascinate me. I'm intrigued by the names, epitaphs, and artwork on the stones. The idyllic settings of many cemeteries appeal to me. I wonder about the history of the burial ground and about the people interred there. My interest began young on my family's occasional weekend outings to explore old graveyards. Now, as I see families pull off the road to take a closer look at a cemetery, I realize many people share this interest.

In the past several years during my travels throughout New Jersey, I have come across many old burial grounds by chance. Each time, I found myself curious about the stories behind the stones. When I looked for books to help me learn more, I found that there were field guides to cemeteries and the graves of famous people for other parts of the country, but none for New Jersey. My goal in writing this book is to help you locate and enjoy old graveyards throughout the state.

Part I of this book gives you general background information about old burial grounds, gravemarker designs, epitaphs, funeral and burial customs, and folklore about New Jersey graveyards.

Part II is a sampler of New Jersey's notable burial grounds, along with advice for making your visits to them enjoyable and safe. The state's Cemetery and Burial Ground Commission has registered thousands of cemeteries, and there are undoubtedly many abandoned ones that never made it into the official records. I have picked out 127 graveyards to describe, some in considerable detail, the rest more briefly, but all are well worth your attention. Before making the final choices, I visited more than two hundred graveyards in all twenty-one counties and took advice from many experts on old cemeteries and on New Jersey history. At the end of the book, I've provided a list of notable burials in New Jersey, suggestions for educational activities, sample forms for recording cemetery and gravestone information, county historical resources, additional sources of help, and a bibliography.

This book concentrates on the earlier burial grounds—ones with gravemarkers dating back to before 1860. I have made a point of choosing burial grounds with gravemarkers that reflect the long complex history of the state. We have the most densely populated state in the union, yet can justly call ourselves the Garden State. Accordingly, I have included burial grounds in the hearts of cities, in the suburbs, and in the countryside.

I especially like to note how cemeteries reflect the ethnic, cultural, and religious diversity of the people who settled New Jersey or chanced to die here. In South Jersey, for example, you can expect to find many English Quaker burial grounds, while in the north, one is more likely to see Moravian, Dutch, Scottish, and German names. But be aware that the graves of many groups of people who lived in New Jersey are not represented here—those whose headstones have not survived, those whose customs or poverty kept them from erecting gravemarkers, and those who arrived in New Jersey after the mid-nineteenth century.

Often gravemarkers are the only evidence we have about early pioneers. The ordinary person living in colonial New Jersey may not be mentioned in a single extant document—no family Bible, church record, or legal papers may have survived—and only the headstone remains to say that this person ever existed. From a few words chiseled into stone, you can glean a whole range of cultural and historical information—and a sudden sense of identification with someone who was once just as alive as you are now.

I hope that this guide will encourage you to explore old burying grounds near your home and throughout the state. As you do, take the time to talk with cemetery caretakers, historians, clergy, genealogists, librarians, archivists, scholars, and amateur "graveyard buffs." As I worked on this guide, they shared their knowledge generously and I am deeply indebted to them for their help. Like everyone who has done research on New Jersey's cemeteries, I am especially grateful to Janet Riemer for her invaluable inventory of over eight hundred burial grounds. If you find yourself becoming deeply interested in the subject, consider joining the New Jersey Graveyard Preservation Society and the Association for Gravestone Studies. Please do send me (in care of the publisher) your comments and further information about early graveyards.

Acknowledgments

I am indebted to so many persons for writing this book. I thank the many historians, professionals, and individuals around the state who offered regional perspectives, namely: William Malloy, Edith Hoelle, Richard Viet, Bob Longcore, Jane Reynolds-Peck, Barbara Carver Smith, Janet Riemer, Claire Bey, Bertha Sheridan, Bill La Rosa, T. Robins Brown, Nancy Shunfenthal, Bob Brooks, Linda Osborne, Ruth Van Wagoner, Wolfgang Albrecht, Jr., Hattie Seiwell, Bob Butcher, Dorothy Stratford, Mark Nonestied, David Heinlein, Hugh Jordan, Nicolas Camaros, Michael Brown, and Gail Greenberg.

I am also grateful to the following persons for allowing me to use their artwork or photographs: Dr. Stanley B. Burns, George H. Moss, Andrea Rhinehart, Lila Sarapin, and Mark Rosenwald.

I thank the friends who shared information, accompanied me on burial-ground visits, and reviewed my writing: Kenneth Rosen, Selena Palmer, Douglas Rhinehart, Patricia Cooper, and Jacqueline Collins; my three children, Lila, Paula, and Joel; my parents, Herbert and Hilda Kohl.

Finally, I thank my editor, Karen Reeds, who gave me the idea and encouragement, based on her own fond memories of visiting burial grounds as a child.

Part One

Old Burial Grounds of New Jersey:

An Introduction

1

Burial Grounds in New Jersey

SCATTERED over the Hagstrom county maps of New Jersey, areas of green mark the locations of cemeteries. They come in all sizes, in many denominations. Some are large, well maintained, with new graves as well as old. Many are tiny, tucked into the corner of the woods, overgrown with weeds. Whether you call them cemeteries, graveyards, burial grounds, or burying grounds, they all hold much of interest to a visitor.

Types of Burial Grounds

New Jersey's earliest burial grounds predate the coming of European settlers. Burial grounds of the Lenni Lenape Indians have been found in Minisink, Indian Mills, Ringwood, and Cape May Court House, to name just a few examples from different parts of the state. Burial grounds were considered sacred. In some tribes, it was the custom to visit the graves once a year to hold a feast and to remove grass from the surrounding area. The graves did not have markers as a rule, although in colonial times white settlers sometimes erected a marker for an Indian who had become a close friend. A few of these markers survive at the sites of the graves of tribal chiefs (see Part II: Hackensack, Flemington, and Burlington).

European settlers first arrived in New Jersey in the late 1600s. The colony had Dutch, English, and German settlements by the early eighteenth century; however, only a few stones marking the graves of settlers from the first half century of colonization have been found. The assumption is that they buried their dead in family plots on their farms and plantations and used simple wood or crude fieldstone markers on the graves.

Today, New Jersey has five kinds of burial grounds that are likely still to have grave markers dating from before 1860.

Family Burial Grounds

Many small family plots remain throughout New Jersey, though today they are hardly used anymore and their very existence may have been forgotten. Some of these family grounds are still cared for by family members or interested individuals and groups. Even in a densely populated state such as New Jersey, hunters or children will still occasionally come across a cluster of gravestones deep in the woods. Contractors are sometimes startled to find skeletons in unmarked graves during excavations. Landowners with old burial grounds on their property have been known to have the remains and stones moved to another burial ground. To locate these family plots—no easy task—consult old local maps and records in historical and genealogical societies.

Denominational Burial Grounds

Thousands of these graveyards can be found throughout the state, and the great majority of the burial grounds described in Part II fall into this category. Most are still associated with a church, temple, or meetinghouse, although the denomination today may be different from the original one, and the original building may long since have been pulled down to make way for a larger one. In some cases, as in Whippany Cemetery and the Old Scots Burial Ground in Marlboro, tombstones going back to the early 1700s remain, but the meetinghouse that once stood beside them (as attested by local documents) disappeared years ago. To find out more about a graveyard associated with a particular religious group or building, first go to the congregation's office. The secretary may be able to direct you to written records or a congregation member who is particularly knowledgeable about its history. The county's and town's historical societies may also be able to help.

Public Burial Grounds

These public cemeteries are not affiliated with religious institutions and are managed today by local governments, parks departments, or historical societies. Some may have started as a small family plot that was later opened to outsiders. Others were "potter's fields," a place to bury people whom no other graveyard would accept. Speer Burial Ground in Jersey City (see Part II) epitomizes the history of such public burial grounds: first, the private plot of a Dutch family in the seventeenth century, then a potter's field, then privately owned by Thomas Speer in the 1850s. From the mid-nineteenth century to the present, Speer burial records are sketchy. Today it is managed by the Hudson County Historical Society.

Commercial Burial Grounds and Memorial Parks

These landscaped park cemeteries became popular in mid-to-late nineteenth- and early twentieth-century New Jersey. Handsome trees, shrubs, and flowers made the cemeteries (which they were more likely to be called than "burial grounds" or graveyards) inviting places to visit. These privately owned cemeteries are typically run for a profit, and they project an image of peaceful, beautiful surroundings. Sometimes these landscaped parks replaced an earlier, abandoned cemetery, as was the case with Trenton's Riverview Cemetery and North Brunswick's Van Liew Cemetery. Both are large and still in use, but also contain older sections with markers dating back to the 1700s. Two exceptionally attractive, well-maintained park cemeteries are Harleigh Cemetery in Camden and Mt. Pleasant Cemetery in Newark.

National Cemeteries

National cemeteries are either located in sites of historical importance or are so designated because prominent colonial citizens or soldiers from many states and different wars are buried there. Two New Jersey cemeteries that have been entered in the National Register of Historical Places are the Evergreen Cemetery in Hillside and Finn's Point National Cemetery (the resting place of many Civil War soldiers and prisoners) near Fort Mott State Park, overlooking the Delaware River and across from the Philadelphia area. Evergreen Cemetery is noted for the graves of such famous writers as Mary Mapes Dodge (*Hans Brinker*), Stephen Crane (*The Red Badge of Courage*), and Edward Stratemeyer (who wrote the Bobbsey Twins series). The Hillside Cemetery also has sections for the graves of orphan children, Gypsies, Jews, and early settlers of various ethnic groups.

Preserving Old Burial Grounds

Like any other sort of property that people use, burial grounds need upkeep. Some of these cemeteries have full-time paid caretakers or part-time park and town employees to take care of the grounds, enforce the graveyard's rules and visiting hours, and protect the graves from vandalism. Others are kept up by family members, volunteers from local scout troops, historical societies, and citizen groups. Others have simply been abandoned.

Since the 1920s, many state statutes have been passed to give graveyards legal protection from the incursions of development. In New Jersey it is illegal to build on top of a burial ground. And a burial ground, by definition, need contain only a single marker and gravesite to become restricted property. Before any development on or around the burial ground is begun, "diligent effort" must be made to locate the owner of the burial property or descendants of the people buried there. Any construction or development nearby must leave the site clearly marked and accessible to descendants. Alternatively, if all the descendants agree, the remains and headstones can be moved to another site. The difficulties of tracking down all the descendants and getting their permission can take years and thwart developers.

The success of these laws can be seen in the examples of small burial plots in the midst of housing developments or shopping malls. The integrity of the original site is maintained, but the juxtaposition of old graveyard and its modern surroundings can be bizarre—as, for example, at the burial ground in the middle of the Route 1 Flea Market (see the section on Ghost Stories and Legends).

Vandalism is a more difficult problem, even though the laws against it are clear. Most cemeteries do not have caretakers on hand at all times. There are, sadly, many examples of the destruction wrought by the callous who steal, deface, and topple stones and even dig up remains. At an old African American burial ground in Fair Haven, for example, headstones mysteriously disappeared between 1990 and 1992; the fact that the land was up for sale made many people suspect that the thefts were somehow related to prospective development. At the Van Campen burial grounds in Pahaquarry, the Mount Prospect Cemetery in Neptune, and a family plot in Carlstadt, stones have vanished in recent years as well. In 1989, townspeople in Carlstadt and descendants of the Outwater family were angered to learn that the skull and some bones of Thomas Fransen Outwater had been stolen from the graveyard and the remaining bones were left exposed (some suspected a satanic cult was responsible for this desecration). Outwater had been one of Bergen County's first freeholders in the 1700s and was buried in this tiny, well-hidden plot in 1761. In a special ceremony for his descendants and local historians, what was left of his remains (the stolen bones and skull were never recovered) was reinterred in July 1990.

New Jersey is not alone in its neglect of old cemeteries and in its problems with vandalism. Throughout the United States, old gravemarkers turn up at antique stores and garage sales. People buy small markers for bookends and mantel-piece decorations. Sometimes the stolen gravestones travel considerable distances: gravestones from Freehold, New Jersey, for example, showed up in Townshend, Vermont. In this case, because the graveyard had already been covered by a development, one of the descendants permitted the stones to be held by the Monmouth County Historical Society for safekeeping. Other cases do not end so amicably. In Hartford, Connecticut, a homeowner in the 1930s built a patio and walkway in his backyard with headstones from a nearby cemetery. The house changed hands in 1990, and city officials were notified about the situation. The new home owner understandably does not want his yard dug up, but the descendants of the people named on the missing markers want the city to return the stones to their proper site. The dispute has not yet been resolved.

Interested citizens, descendants of early settlers and Revolutionary War soldiers, county historical associations, county cultural and heritage commissions, volunteer organizations, genealogical societies, and religious institutions have long been involved in preserving old New Jersey burial grounds. Their activities include placing new markers on the gravesites of historical figures, photographing markers, transcribing inscriptions, and restoring fragile tombstones. A particularly noteworthy inventory of the state's cemeteries was undertaken in 1988 by Janet T. Riemer for the New Jersey Genealogical Society. Her index of over eight hundred burial grounds at the Alexander Library at Rutgers University includes fourteen file drawers of cards with transcriptions of gravestones, arranged alphabetically by surname.

2
Burying the Dead

IN CONTEMPORARY America, the topic of how to dispose of our bodily remains is as taboo as the subject of death itself. We are reluctant to talk about our preferences for burial or cremation, for a simple funeral or an elaborate one—as if by speaking about death, we may bring it on. Unlike past generations, many Americans today grow up without ever going to a funeral, without having a playmate or sibling die in childhood. In a mobile society, many people may not know where their ancestors and kinfolk are buried.

For many parents today, children's questions about death are more difficult and dismaying to answer than questions about sex. So children draw their own conclusions. In their minds, cemeteries are not associated with weekly visits to the family burial plot, but with a jumble of misinformation drawn from movies, ghost stories, and superstitions. When I was a child, for example, I learned that walking over a grave would bring bad luck; that at night unhappy ghosts roam about the headstones, moaning and rattling their chains; that at full moon vampires, mummies, the undead, witches, skeletons, and ghouls would rise up out of the graves. More recently, I have seen a whole carload of children holding their breath while driving by a cemetery, fearing to breathe in the spirits of the dead. Youngsters still dare each other to walk through cemeteries after dark, especially at Halloween.

Modern American culture has pushed the dead farther and farther away from the living. But it was not always so. In the early 1800s, an American child had only a 50 percent chance of reaching adulthood. Smallpox, measles, diphtheria, scarlet fever, and malaria devastated families and communities. In all age groups, death was an everyday occurrence, but no less sorrowful for its familiarity. The all-too-common rituals of burying the dead, raising gravestones, and visiting graves helped the survivors ease their grief, remember their loved ones, and prepare for their own ends. If we know something about those earlier customs of burying the dead, we can understand better what we see in old graveyards now.

Funeral and Burial Customs

Funerals and gravestones reflected the status of the dead and the aspirations of the living. An important person would be buried with great pomp. The family might send out black "mourning gloves" for friends and kin as invitations to the funeral and distribute printed, black-bordered funeral cards with a short biography of the deceased. The mourners would gather to deliver eulogies over the casket and to form a slow procession from the church or home to the place of burial. The horses that carried the coffin might wear black plumes and cloths embroidered with skulls on their heads and black stockings around their legs. Close friends and family would feel honored to receive clippings of the dead person's hair, to be placed in mourning rings, pins, and lockets as lasting mementos.

A young child would be laid to rest with much less ceremony. The parents might put in the casket a doll or homemade toy or a piece of jewelry. The tombstone and inscription would be modest, often just the child's name and dates of birth and death and a simple expression of grief.

To keep memories alive, especially of a young woman or a child, very wealthy families in Europe and colonial America sometimes commissioned postmortem likenesses: paintings of the dead person with symbols of death—stopped clocks or flowers—in otherwise typical family settings.

After 1839, daguerrotypes replaced the postmortem paintings and made it possible for ordinary people to put pictures of their loved ones on the graves, a custom still occasionally practiced. These early photographs would be displayed in special holders attached to the tombstones. Often the photograph would have been taken while the person was still alive, but it became an important and accepted custom to use postmortem photographs, especially when a child had died. Because the eyes of the corpse were usually left open and the picture was taken in natural poses, it is not always easy to tell whether the photograph was taken before or after death. The parents, dressed in black, wearing funeral gloves, and

1. A funeral card for Mrs. Mollie R. Logan (d. November 6, 1887).

2. A stereoview of mourners and gravestones at Tennent Church Cemetery, by
Luther R. Cheeseman of Trenton, probably late 1860s. (Courtesy of George Moss,
from his book, *Double Exposure*, Ploughshare Press, 1971, p. 93.)

surrounded by flowers, might hold their dead child. Or a young man or
woman would be shown lying on a couch or bed, seemingly at rest.
Rarely, the photograph would be taken at the grave, with the corpse lying
in the coffin. (Stanley Burns's collection of postmortem photographs, in
his book *Sleeping Beauties,* gives a fascinating glimpse into this custom.)

In the mid- and late nineteenth century and into the early twentieth,
as cemeteries came to look more and more like parks, photographers discovered a demand for pictures of burial grounds, notable gravemarkers,
and churches—a natural extension of the interest in photographs of all
kinds of outdoor landscapes. In the late nineteenth century, scenes of
graveyards were sold as sets of stereocards for viewing through a stere-
opticon; in the early twentieth century postcards of cemeteries became
popular. Stereocard series of New Jersey burial grounds include Luther
Cheeseman's photographs of Tennent Church and R. H. Rose's series of
the College of New Jersey graveyard.

Arrangements of Burial Grounds

Just as funeral customs took account of status, symbolism, and tradition,
so did the graveyards. The older burial grounds generally followed the
configuration of European churchyards. Bodies were buried horizontally,
to "sleep" until the Day of Resurrection. The bodies lay oriented east-west,

3. The photograph of Esther Lebowitz (d. 1934), displayed on her tombstone in an old Jewish cemetery on Route 34 in Matawan.

4. A postmortem photograph of a young girl. (From *Sleeping Beauty: A History of Memorial Photography in America*, Altadena, Calif.: Twelvetrees Press, 1990; collection of Stanley B. Burns, M.D.)

with the feet pointing to the east, in accordance with the Christian belief that on Judgment Day, the Angel Gabriel would appear in the east and the spirits of the dead would rise from the graves, all facing east. Out of respect for the dead, the gravestone would bear an inscription on the side facing away from the body, so that someone reading the epitaph would not walk over the grave mound. Sometimes an additional smaller stone would mark the foot of the grave (these footstones are easily confused with small gravemarkers of children and servants).

The oldest burials in a graveyard were typically closest to the first structure, the meetinghouse or church, sometimes even leaning against its walls. (If the building has been renovated or replaced, the rule may not hold true.) When additions were made to churches to accommodate a growing population, the new walls were often built right over existing graves. In colonial times it was taken as a special honor to be buried inside the church (to be buried under the altar carried the most prestige; next

5. A stereoview of the gravestone for Aaron Burr (b. 1756, d. 1836), Princeton Cemetery, Princeton, by R. H. Rose, probably late 1870s. Burr was vice president of the United States, 1801–1805, and notorious for killing Alexander Hamilton in a duel in Weehawken, New Jersey, on July 11, 1804. (Hamilton was buried in Trinity Church Burial Ground, New York City.) (Author's collection.)

best was under the floor of the nave or aisles), so you will often find the graves of ministers and church leaders inside the building. Sometimes the gravestone of someone buried in the church will be embedded in the sides of the church itself, another sign of honor. (See, for example, St. Mary's Church in Burlington.)

A monument will sometimes commemorate a person who is buried elsewhere or whose body was never found. These cenotaphs (from a Greek word meaning "empty tomb") are common in graveyards along the Jersey shore, where they honor men and women who were lost at sea. A grieving widow in Atlantic County, for example, erected a marble cenotaph in Head of the River Cemetery that read simply:

John B. Willets
Lost at sea—My husband!

It is interesting to look for graves of members of a single family and to try to trace their relationships from the arrangement of the stones and inscriptions. As a rule, family members are buried next to each other in a

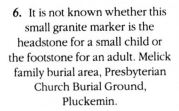

6. It is not known whether this small granite marker is the headstone for a small child or the footstone for an adult. Melick family burial area, Presbyterian Church Burial Ground, Pluckemin.

7a. Tombstones embedded in the sides of Old St. Mary's Church, Burlington.

7b. Gravemarkers for the young men sent by the government of Japan in the late nineteenth century to study in American colleges and universities. Willow Grove Cemetery, New Brunswick.

single plot, sometimes with a low wall or wrought-iron fence surrounding the graves. A line of smaller stones by a pair of larger stones is enough to tell the sad story of a family whose children died before the parents. The sight of a tiny stone, perhaps with no name or even initials, next to the tomb of a young woman reminds us of the thousands of mothers who died in childbirth and of the babies who did not long survive them. It is not uncommon to see the grave of a man flanked by the stones of his first wife on one side and his second on the other.

Look too for groupings of graves—of men who died in a Revolutionary War battle or of victims of an epidemic, for example. You may be able to detect more subtle patterns: a preponderance of deaths among a particular age group, or among immigrants from one country. A distinctive cluster of gravestones in Willow Grove Cemetery in New Brunswick, for example, commemorates eight young Japanese men who died in this country while studying at Rutgers and other American colleges, members of a select group sent by the Japanese government in the late nineteenth century.

The outcasts of a community might be buried on the edges of the graveyard or in a separate potter's field. Some faiths forbade the burial of suicides in consecrated ground. Because towns were reluctant to spend money on stones for paupers, criminals, ne'er-do-wells, and people without families, these graves are especially hard to identify. Occasionally, authorities might require the corpse of someone who died of infectious disease to be buried secretly at night or far away from the local cemetery.

3

Gravemarkers and Inscriptions

WALK THROUGH an old burying ground and inevitably you'll find yourself looking at individual stones, your eye caught by a curious carving or half-readable inscription. As you look at many gravemarkers, you will begin to see patterns of designs and epitaphs.

Kinds of Gravemarkers

The carved stone gravemarkers from the seventeenth, eighteenth, and early nineteenth centuries in an old New Jersey burial ground represent only part of the gravemarkers that were set up in the early days of the colony and state. From surviving documents, we know that the earliest markers were often made from wood or common fieldstone.

The wooden markers were carved from local trees, for example from red cedar in South Jersey. Very few of these survive. The only one I have seen is at Cold Spring burial ground in Cape May County. It is about three feet tall, of a rough texture, like driftwood, and unremarkable in shape or appearance. The inscription has long since weathered away. Today it is attached to the wall inside the caretaker's office and can be seen only by permission. If it were left outside, the odds are it would be taken by a souvenir hunter or blown away by high winds in a coastal storm. To judge from this marker, it is possible that other wooden markers survive in New Jersey that simply have not been recognized as such because they are so crudely shaped.

Fieldstone markers were more durable. Thousands can be found throughout the state, but because most lack inscriptions, it is hard to know just how old they are. Jersey City, Middletown, Crosswicks, Perth Amboy,

Elizabeth, Newark, Woodbridge, Mahwah, and Edison all have good, early examples. These early gravestones were taken from fields or woods, rather than quarried, and put up in their original shapes. The fieldstone markers rarely have more than initials and dates carved on them, and those brief inscriptions are very crudely done. Otherwise, they were left uncarved because of local custom, because of religious belief, because local artisans lacked skills and tools to work the stones, or because they marked the grave of a person of little standing in the community: an indentured servant, a slave, or a pauper.

The old stone markers that catch our eye in graveyards are made of marble, sandstone, slate, and granite. (Occasionally, we may be fooled by a dark brown, reddish, or even green marker that turns out to be made not of stone, but of iron or, less often, bronze.) Before 1850, sandstone and marble were most commonly used. The stone was either quarried within the state or imported from Pennsylvania, New York, or Connecticut. Very rarely, an unusual design or kind of stone suggests that the marker came from overseas; the Presbyterian Burial Ground in Middletown, for example, has a stone that is thought to have been shipped from England (see Part II).

Sandstone was the most popular choice for gravestones. Deposits were conveniently available along the banks of New Jersey rivers such as the Raritan, Mullica, and Delaware; New York and New Jersey stonecarvers liked to use sandstone from Newark and the lower Hudson valley. Equally important, the soft sedimentary rock was easy to carve. New Jersey sandstone markers vary in color from shades of reddish brown to white, depending on the minerals present in the rock.

Marble was more expensive, harder to obtain, and more difficult to carve than sandstone, but it had other attractions: a statuary tradition reaching back to ancient Greece and Rome, a hardness that allowed for intricate details and delicate designs, and a range of beautiful colors. The metamorphic rock had to be quarried outside the state and brought in by boat or wagon. In colonial New Jersey, marble was used for the graves and memorials of soldiers, civic and religious leaders, and statesmen. The larger box tombs and taller monuments were almost always carved from marble. Good examples include the row of impressive marble-topped tombs (built on a brick base) of all but four of the past presidents of Princeton University in Princeton Cemetery and the monument of Elias

8. A stereoview of Presidents' Plot, where eleven presidents of Princeton University are buried, by R. H. Rose, probably late 1870s. Princeton Cemetery, Princeton. (Author's collection.)

Boudinot, statesman, clergyman, and president of the American Bible Society, in St. Mary's Churchyard in Burlington.

A smaller proportion of New Jersey's gravestones were carved from granite, a common igneous rock with a coarse texture and colors ranging from brown to tan, with stripes or speckles from bits of mica, orthoclase, and quartz embedded in the rock. Granite was quarried in the Ramapo Mountains in northern New Jersey and imported from the Catskills and the mountains of New England.

Slate, a metamorphic rock produced from clay and shale, was used for some New Jersey gravestones. The dark gray stones tended to split into layers and thus did not survive very well. Examples can be found in the Presbyterian Churchyard in New Providence.

"White bronze" (actually zinc) markers are most common in South Jersey cemeteries, although they can be found in other places (for example, Bevans Burial Ground in Sussex County). Apparently, the South Jersey markers were shipped from Philadelphia. These markers look as if they are made of white marble, but the hollow sound you get on tapping them gives away their true material. Their ornate designs and plaques were cast separately and attached to the body of the marker later on.

Preserving Gravemarkers

The composition of the stone and its exposure to the elements determine how well a gravemarker lasts over time and how well its inscription can be read years after it was erected. Markers on high hills, exposed to strong winds, rain, and extreme temperatures are, not surprisingly, more likely to crumble or lose their outer layers than more sheltered stones. Conversely, gravemarkers covered by dead leaves, vines, or layers of lichen last longer than markers out in the open. (If you are cleaning a graveyard, ask a plant expert to examine the grounds: clearing away vegetation may do more harm than good to the gravestone.) But, sadly, human vandalism is more likely to damage a stone than weathering.

The restoration of old tombstones is an expensive and difficult task. The markers need to be regarded as a class of fragile stone sculptures that

9. Neglect of New Brunswick's Willow Grove Cemetery allowed a tree to grow around the gravemarker of Mary, the daughter of Stephen and Letitia Fitzrandolph. The tree's bark conceals the date of death.

require special techniques to keep them from falling over or weathering away. Sometimes, well-meaning attempts to save tombstones have only subjected them to greater harm. For example, using concrete to encase tombstones, especially the more porous sandstone markers, can trap mineral salts from the concrete, which speeds up the deterioration of the old stone. Cleaning off dirt and lichen with a stiff brush—once the recommended method for making it easier to read an inscription—will expose the marker to the elements and wear down the surface of stones. Taking rubbings of the carvings, a popular practice in the 1960s, can also damage the stones if done improperly, and many burial grounds now forbid the practice. Exposure to the weather, polluted air, and acid rain are bad enough for stones without someone rubbing away the design and lettering as well. Straightening gravestones that have tilted or fallen over also requires special techniques. In trying to set a stone upright, people often apply too much pressure and end up breaking it off; they have forgotten to allow for the part of the stone that extends as much as three feet under ground.

Often the best way to save an old stone from all these hazards is to cast a duplicate stone to set at the gravesite and put the original inside a building for safekeeping. If you are interested in trying to protect or restore a tombstone, consult an expert recommended by the nationally known group, the Association for Gravestone Studies (see Appendix 6, Additional Sources).

The Stonecarvers

Carving a gravestone required special skills and tools. Often the stonecarver did the work as a sideline to carpentry or masonry; for some, it was a full-time occupation. When we see particularly rough lettering, misspellings, uneven spacing, and very simple designs, we can suspect that the stone was carved by someone with no training in the craft. Most stonecarvers have remained anonymous, although we can sometimes trace their work through distinctive motifs, designs, letter forms, or even characteristic misspellings.

We do know the names of several stonecarvers who were active in central to northern New Jersey in the late 1700s and early 1800s, and

10. Gravestone cut and signed by Abner Stewart, apprentice of Ebenezer Price,
marking the grave of Daniel Sale (d. 1798, age seventy-three). First Presbyterian
Church Burial Ground, Elizabeth. (Courtesy Emily Wasserman,
Gravestone Designs, Rubbings, and Photographs from Early New York and New Jersey.
New York: Dover Publications, 1972.)

examples of their work can be found in many old graveyards in that re-
gion. They include Henry Osborne of Woodbridge, Jonathan Hand Os-
borne of Scotch Plains, J. C. Mooney of Connecticut Farms (Union), Uzal
Ward of Newark, Isaac and Aaron Ross and L. and Henry Silcocks of New
Brunswick, John Frazee of Rahway, John Zuricher and Thomas Brown of
Manhattan, and Ebenezer Price of Elizabeth and his three assistants, Abner
Stewart, Jonathan Akin, and David Jeffries (of Woodbridge).

Jonathan Hand Osborne and Henry Osborne both signed markers in
the years spanning 1770 to 1810. Although they shared the same last name,
it is not known whether they were related. Jonathan Hand Osborne, the
son of a tavern keeper, learned his trade in his late twenties. He signed his
stones at the top, perhaps as advertising. Henry Osborne generally signed

his stones as H.O. or H. Osborne at the bottom and added a gentle tulip motif. The work of both stonecarvers can be found on stones in Springfield, Union, Elizabeth, Spotswood, Cranbury, Scotch Plains, as well as in Richmondtown on Staten Island.

The reputations of some stonecarvers brought them commissions from a wide region. John Zuricher, for example, had a shop in Manhattan where he carved hundreds of sandstone markers from the 1740s until the Revolutionary War. When the British occupied Manhattan, Zuricher, a Tory sympathizer, fled to his son's farm in Rockland County and kept on carving. His gravestones can be found in Middletown (see fig. 60), Mahwah, Elizabeth, New York City, as well as in Rockland County. Zuricher's

11. The distinctive style of Ebenezer Price's carving appears in the soul effigy, tulip motif, and crossed bones on this gravemarker for David Maxsell, "who died of yᵉ Small Pox by innoculation" (1763). Connecticut Farms Presbyterian Burial Ground, Union.

own burying place has never been located. Stones in New Jersey and New York by another Manhattan carver, Thomas Brown, can be identified by his unique mortality symbol (see, for example, the John Downey stone in the Christ Episcopal Church Graveyard, New Brunswick, fig. 56). A delicate cherub (found on stones in Matawan and Middletown) is also indicative of Brown's work. John Frazee of New Brunswick, a well-known sculptor, was occasionally commissioned to do tombstones; examples of his carvings can be found in the South River Cemetery in Middlesex County.

The gravestones carved by Ebenezer Price and his assistants Akin, Stewart, and Jeffries in the mid- to late 1700s show how styles could be passed along from master carver to apprentice. Jeffries learned his trade from Price, and both specialized in effigies of the soul, depicted with full cheeks, deep-set eyes, and oval braided hair. The two carvers also often used a tulip motif, rather like a fleur-de-lis, at the top of tombstones. Their carvings can be found in burial grounds in northern and central New Jersey: Elizabeth, Union, Woodbridge, and Spotswood, among others.

The value of distinctive motifs in tracing the work of a single carver is demonstrated by half a dozen gravestones, all dated between 1781 and 1785, in three different cemeteries. These stones by an anonymous artisan all bear round-faced soul effigies, with almond-shaped eyes and long noses. The gravestones were for Caty Leonard (First Presbyterian Church-

12. The almond-shaped eyes and round faces are characteristic of the gravestones made by an anonymous stonecarver between 1781 and 1785. Stone for Caty Leonard (d. 1789, age twenty-four). Presbyterian Burial Grounds, Middletown. (Courtesy Emily Wasserman, *Gravestone Designs, Rubbings, and Photographs from Early New York and New Jersey,* New York: Dover Publications, 1972.)

yard, Middletown, New Jersey), James Bryant, Elizabeth Halliker, and Josh Mooney (St. Paul's Churchyard, New York City), and Harman Carpenter and Sarah/John Venning (Trinity Church Burial Ground, New York City).

Designs and Motifs

Make a point of noticing the shapes of gravestones as well as the designs carved on them. Most gravemarkers are simple rectangular slabs and have nothing beyond the name of the person who died, dates, and perhaps a brief inscription. That may have been all the family could afford, all the local artisan was capable of carving, or all the religious tradition permitted. But those stones that do have carvings have their own stories to tell.

Although some designs were certainly requested by the bereaved family, the shape of the marker and its design could also be determined by what was available. During slack times, professional stonecarvers would cut stones to size and incise popular motifs. When a death occurred, a member of the family could visit the shop and choose from the partly prepared stones on hand. The family would specify the wording of an inscription, and the carver would finish the stone and have it delivered to the gravesite. Stonecarvers with more than a local reputation, like John Zuricher in Manhattan, might get orders by letter or messenger.

Although the designs found on early New Jersey gravemarkers bear strong resemblances to those of New England, New York, and Long Island graveyards of the same periods, there are some interesting differences— determined both by the choice of material and by religious belief—to look out for. The native New Jersey sandstone and limestone does not allow the sharp detail possible with the harder granite, schist, and slate of New England. So gravestones of the harder stone and more ornate carvings are likely to have been imported from outside New Jersey—a sign of the family's wealth or their love and respect for the person who died.

The variety of symbolism on New Jersey gravestones (and differences around the state) reflects the diversity of religious beliefs among New Jersey settlers. Indeed, many who left New England and Pennsylvania in search of religious tolerance found it in New Jersey. Crosses are common motifs on the gravestones of Christians (especially Lutherans, Presbyterians, and Roman Catholics), and six-sided stars on stones of

Table 1 ❧ *Symbolism of Common Motifs on New Jersey Gravestones*

Motif	Symbolic Meaning
Anchor	Grave of a seafarer reaching final haven, cross
Angel	Afterlife in heaven, heavenly messenger
Bird, dove	Purity, youthfulness, Holy Spirit, flight to heaven
Bones, crossed	Death of the body
Buds	Renewal of life, life cut short
Cherub	Childlike innocence, divine wisdom, death of child
Coffin	Mortality
Cradle	Death of baby
Crown	Placed on soul effigy to honor goodness of character
Effigy	Image of spirit of the deceased
Flowers	Respect, beauty, sorrow, life cut off before maturity
Gun, sword, cannon	Grave of a soldier
Hands	Prayer, devotion, farewell to mortal life
Heart	Eternal life
Hourglass	Life has run out of time on earth, warning of little time left
Lamb	Innocence (usually for child)
Scythe	Time passing, death cutting off life
Sheaves of wheat	The final harvest
Ship	Seafarer's grave
Skull, death's head	Death of the body
Thistle	Grave of a Scot, remembrance
Tree	Tree of life
Tree fallen, branch broken	Life and growth cut off by death
Vine	Intertwining of soul with God
Willows	Sorrow, weeping with grief
Wings	Flight of spirit

Jews. The influence of Quakers in many parts of southern New Jersey (and to a lesser degree in the north), for example, may be revealed in a preference for simple, small gravemarkers, with no more than names or initials chiseled into the stone. The Puritan influence shows up in early carvings of death's heads. Gravestones have their fashions like everything else, and it is interesting to see how the grim Puritan symbols give way to other, gentler motifs of angels, soul effigies, willows, urns, flowers, and gesturing hands, or to more worldly designs to commemorate the dead person's profession in life. See Table 1 for a list of other motifs and designs found on New Jersey gravestones.

Death's Heads and Soul Effigies

A common motif on pre-1750 gravemarkers (especially, but not exclusively, in Presbyterian churchyards) is a skull, with bones crossed beneath it. This piece of Puritan symbolism, more common in New England than in New Jersey, reminds the onlooker of the mortality of the body. Several graveyards described in Part II have good examples: Elizabeth (First Presbyterian), Woodbridge (First Presbyterian), Perth Amboy (St. Peter's Episcopal). A variation—crossed bones without the skull—can be seen in Marlboro (Old Scots Cemetery). A unique variant in the graveyard of Christ Episcopal Church, New Brunswick, shows the large crossed bones on top, and underneath, a serpent bent into a circle to bite its tail, an ancient symbol of eternity (see fig. 56).

Between 1730 and 1770, another version of the skull became popular on tombstones in central and northern New Jersey: the death's head with its deep eye sockets, prominent nose bridge, and rectangular teeth. A downward slant to the eyes or mouth added to the gloomy aspect of these effigies. Wings to the sides of the death's head underscored the Puritan belief that flight from death, sin, and damnation was impossible.

13. Death's head and crossed bones on the gravestone of Gertrude Hay (d. 1733, age forty-seven). St. Peter's Episcopal Church Burial Ground, Perth Amboy.

14. Winged death's head on the gravestone of Benjamin Disbrow (d. 1733). Old Tennent Church Cemetery, Tennent.

As the strict Puritan doctrine loosened its grasp, a new symbol began to appear on gravestones (between 1750 and 1820): the ascending angel or soul, representing the hope of resurrection. Sometimes the souls wear crowns, signs of their noble character in life, or their rewards in heaven. The epitaphs that accompany these carvings often mention the hope of reuniting with the loved one in an afterlife. The features on the faces of the souls are often round, cherubic—as on the stone of Samuel Tuttle in Whippany Cemetery (see Part II). A fascinating touch is the treatment of the hair, curled after the fashion of eighteenth-century wigs.

Willows, Urns, and Flowers

The graceful willow tree began to appear on New Jersey headstones in the early 1800s and became very common in the 1840s. The willow represented the weeping and sorrow of the bereft survivors, an ancient symbol of mourning whose meaning was intertwined with the biblical symbolism of the Tree of Life. A good example of the willow tree design is on markers for the Conover family, in Tennent Presbyterian Burial Ground (see Part II). Sometimes the willow tree is accompanied by a box tomb on one side of the tree, and a lone bud on the other—a reminder of a person who had died in the bloom of life.

During the Victorian era, funeral urns became a favorite symbol, ei-

15. Willows on headstones of Rebecca Conover (d. 1859) and her husband, Peter Conover (d. 1860). Old Tennent Church Cemetery, Tennent.

16. Shaped like a funeral urn, the gravestone of General L. M. Pine (d. 1815 at York, Upper Canada) is embedded in a wall of St. Michael's Church, Trenton. When the church's walls were extended in 1846, his grave remained under the church floor and his stone was placed in the wall nearby.

ther as a carving or as the shape of the tombstone itself. (A few examples are known from the eighteenth century.) The tombstone of Anthony Parker, buried in Lanoka Harbor (see Part II) in 1851, for example, shows a funerary urn draped with a shroud. An urn-shaped tombstone is embedded in the wall of St. Michael's Church in Trenton.

Flowers, buds, and thistles were frequent motifs on markers throughout the state. Again, the flower or bud symbolized the brevity of life, the contrast of life and death in nature, frequently on the gravestones of children or young men and women. A touching example for an adult is the bouquet tipped on the ground, depicted on the marker of Annie Claypoole, who died in 1871 in Cape May County at the age of forty-five. The thistle is a symbol of remembrance to the living (although it can also refer to Scottish ancestry).

Hands

Hands were a common symbol on gravestones in the mid- and late nineteenth century, and they are often coupled with epitaphs praising the goodness of the person buried there. Hands are usually shown in prayer,

17. The gravestone of Annie Claypoole (d. 1871, age forty-five) with an overturned basket of flowers. Fairview Methodist Burial Ground, Cape May Court House.

18. An interesting hand motif on the gravestone of Selah O. Soper (d. 1863). Sea Captain's Cemetery, Barnegat.

as a symbol of the dead person's piety. Two hands clasping or shaking each other was both a symbol of farewell on earth and a reminder that the dead and living would meet again in heaven. A hand with the index finger pointing upward (see fig. 36) turned the bystander's thoughts toward heaven, where the spirit of the dead had ascended.

Symbols of Occupations

Given New Jersey's 127 miles of coastline, it is no surprise to find the graves or memorials of hundreds of sailors and sea captains in the state's burial grounds. Their stones often have carvings of ships or anchors. An anchor symbolizes both a safe haven and, in its shape, the cross; the anchor motif may also invoke the scriptural description of faith as an anchor of the soul. Look in the cemeteries in South Jersey for the marble markers commemorating seafarers and shipwrecked passengers.

Guns and swords on a gravestone indicate the resting place of a

19. An anchor on the gravestone of Captain Charles Soper (d. 1904). Barnegat Cemetery, Barnegat.

soldier, although not necessarily one who died in battle. These motifs are common on stones in Elizabeth, Springfield, and Connecticut Farms (Union), the sites of Revolutionary War battles.

The image of an open book carved on a gravestone may signify a scholar or teacher, although the motif can also evoke the more strictly religious meaning of the Bible, the Torah, or the Book of Judgment. Religious leaders were often honored by especially ornate tombstones with large crosses, if Christian, or a Star of David or Torah, if Jewish.

20. John Voorhies (presumably a blacksmith) and his strong right arm are strikingly commemorated on this stone (date of death illegible). First Presbyterian Burial Ground, Cranbury.

Epitaphs

Through epitaphs, the dead speak to the living. Visitors to old graveyards are often struck by directness and emotion of the inscriptions, so unlike the reticence of modern epitaphs. The epitaphs do not hesitate to remind us: *Here Lyes Yᵉ Body*—someone's remains really do lie below this stone. *Memento Mori,* "Remember Death," the old Latin warning of our own mortality, has not lost its power to shock, even three centuries later.

To appreciate early epitaphs, it helps to know some of the conventions and changes in written language (lexicology is the technical word for this) in the seventeenth and eighteenth centuries (see table 2). In the common phrase, *Here Lyes Yᵉ Body,* for example, *Yᵉ* does not mean the old form of the pronoun, *you,* but it is rather an old scribal abbreviation for *the.* The diphthong, *th,* was replaced by an Anglo-Saxon letter named *thorn,* which was shaped somewhat like the Roman letter *Y* and pronounced *th.* For the stonecarver (or printer, or sign painter), the *thorn* abbreviation and the superscript *e* gave some flexibility in spacing letters and words to make lines come out even.

Another convention to watch out for as you read or transcribe epitaphs is the use of the "long s." The letter is pronounced *s,* but it looks very much like a lower-case flowing *f,* without the crossbar (or the crossbar only extending to the left). It is easily misread as an *f.* You will not find the "long s" used to write an initial *s* sound; it comes later in a word, often

Table 2 ❧ **Chronological Lexicology for New Jersey Gravemarker**

Phrase	Period
Lyes ye body . . . Lyeth the body . . . Here lies interred . . .	Late 1600s
Here lies the mortal part . . . Here lies interred the body of . . . Here lies the body of . . .	Early 1700s
Here rests in God . . . Died . . . Sacred to the memory of . . . Erected in memory of . . . In hope of a joyful resurrection	Mid-1700s
In memory of . . .	Late 1700s and early 1800s, and ever since

as the first *s* in a pair. (Both the *thorn* and the "long s" dropped out of common usage in written English in the late 1700s; nowadays, they are used only for comic or old-fashioned effect.)

Sometimes a woman's epitaph will call her "consort." This meant "spouse" and had no pejorative connotation. The word "mistress"—which came to be abbreviated as Mrs.—simply meant "wife." Similarly, "relict" meant "widow."

Spelling, punctuation, and capitalization on gravestones in colonial New Jersey were no more standardized than in any other written matter of the day—Noah Webster's dictionary, the first attempt to regularize American English, was not published until 1828. Early settlers often arrived with little formal schooling or books save perhaps a family Bible. Ordinary words might be spelled several ways within an inscription. Family names on gravemarkers were especially prone to have variant spellings: a member of the bereaved family might make a mistake while spelling out the name of the deceased for an inscription, or the stonecarver might have misheard the name.

Consider, for example, the Dutch name Van Wagenen. This appears as Van Wagon, Van Wagenon, Van Wagenen, and Van Wagonen in various New Jersey graveyards. Because the prefix *Van* in Dutch names means the person came from a particular area of the Netherlands, we cannot even be sure that all the Van Wagenens named on these gravemarkers are related. An extra piece of lexicological information to be considered with Dutch names is that women often retained their birth names after marriage and on their tombstones.

The most interesting epitaphs are those that go beyond the simple facts of name, age, and date. Sometimes it is an admonition to the living that impresses us—a frequent theme of epitaphs in the eighteenth and nineteenth centuries:

> Stop my friend! O take another view!
> The dust that molders here
> Was once belov'd like you!
> No longer then on future time rely
> Improve the present
> and prepare to die!
> *(Epitaph for Hannah Crane, died 1852 at age 45,*
> *First Presbyterian Burial Ground, Elizabeth)*

> I have left you, no more my pale face to see,
> Prepare Yourselves to follow me
> *(Epitaph for Anna Aires, died July 1828 at age twenty-five,*
> *North Woodbury Burial Ground)*

> In Memory of Captain Abraham
> Tappen who deceased Sept 29, 1799
> in the 43rd year of his age
> Be ye also ready for in such an hour as ye think not
> The fall of man cometh
> *(First Presbyterian Burial Ground, Woodbridge)*

An inscription from 1798 makes the point in words of one syllable:

> As you are now, So once was I
> In Health & Strength, tho here I lie
> As I am now, So must you be
> Prepare for Death & follow me.
> *(Daniel Sale, died at age seventy-three,*
> *First Presbyterian Burial Ground, Elizabeth)*

Occasionally, an epitaph seems almost ghoulish in making the contrast between decaying flesh and the resurrected spirit:

Let worms devour my roasting flesh
And crumble all my bones to dust:
My God shall raise my frame anew
At the revival of the just
(Thomas Speer, died 1829 at age seventy-eight,
Fairfield Reformed Church Burial Ground)

Sometimes a personality suddenly comes alive in the inscription, as in this tribute to a much-beloved wife, Sarah Ann (no married name given):

Sarah Ann daughter of Arch and Phoebe Stewart
who fell a victim to a relentless fever at Perth Amboy
on 27th April, 1814, age 34. She was tenderly
affectionate, truly benevolent, pious and devout,
just, charitable and humane, the steady friend of the
needy and afflicted, and a true believer in
a redeemers love. To her memory this monument is
erected as the last tribute of respect by a husband
who will never cease to mourn her loss on earth, and
whose hope is a final reunion in heaven.
(Hackettstown Presbyterian Church Burial Ground)

The grief of parents for their children comes through poignantly in this stoic epitaph in South Jersey:

Our Life is ever on the wing,
And death is ever nigh
The moment when our lives begin
We all begin to die
(Reuben Townsend, died 1812 at age fourteen,
Seaville Methodist Churchyard)

And in this verse which combines so many images of a life ended all too early:

Death like an overflowing stream
Sweeps away our life, a dream
An empty tale, a mourning flower
Cut down and withered in an hour.
(Samuel Harriot, died 1808 at age nine,
Woodbridge First Presbyterian Burial Ground)

From epitaphs, the hazards of life in early America come through vividly. The victim of one of the smallpox epidemics that swept across the state in the late 1700s and early 1800s, for example, is remembered in this inscription in the St. James Burial Ground, Edison:

> Here Lyes the body of Elizabeth
> FitzRandolph died March y^c 19
> 1792 Aged 43 years daught of
> Thomas died with y^c small pox.

An epitaph can give us a sharp vignette of another era, as in these records of sudden death:

> William Christie, native of Scotland
> late merchant of Philadelphia who was
> cut off in the flower of his youth by falling from a
> stagecoach near Cranbury on Oct 24, 1796 and was
> killed on the spot.
> *(Cranbury, First Presbyterian Burial Ground; see fig. 53)*

> That Cherry Tree of luscious fruit
> Beguiled him too high, a branch did break
> and down he fell and broke his neck and
> died July 13th, 1862.
> *(Andrew C. Hand, Mt. Pleasant Cemetery, Newark)*

> John M. Roof, born in Canajoharie, NY. Was acting as
> an assistant to the engineer in exploring the route
> for the Morris Canal and died at Hackettstown, b Nov
> 24, 1805 d Sept 17, 1823.
> *(Hackettstown Presbyterian Burial Ground)*

Epitaphs in burial grounds near battlefields remind us of the deaths of individual soldiers, both of Americans and of British and Hessians killed far from home. This epitaph for a Revolutionary War soldier killed by Hessians in 1780 at the Battle of Connecticut Farms (now known as Union) brings alive the patriotic fervor that kept Americans fighting against the odds:

> Behold Me here as you Pass By
> Who bled and Dy'd for Liberty
> From British Tyrents now am free.
> *(Nicholas Parcell, Short Hills)*

Soldiers who survived the war often made a point of their military service in their epitaphs years later:

> Sacred to the memory of Joel Fithian
> Who departed from this life November 9, 1821 in the
> 71 year of his age. He was a soldier in the Revolution
> and served his Country in many important offices
> and the Church in Greenwich as a Ruling Elder with
> zeal and fidelity. Reader imitate his virtues that
> your end like his be peaceful.
> *(Presbyterian Church Burial Ground, Greenwich)*

If an epitaph on a gravestone makes you curious about the person buried beneath it, transcribe the epitaph carefully and use it as the starting point for an adventure in historical detective work. First, look around the graveyard for the stones of other people with the same family name or who lived at about the same time, and take down their epitaphs as well. Then turn to the records of the graveyard, the group that maintains it, local libraries, town and state archives, and historical and genealogical societies. Even if your search through old books, diaries, deeds, wills, and maps turns up little information about the person in the epitaph, you will have your reward: the world of the past will come alive for you and you will always have a sense of kinship to those people long dead.

4

Ghost Stories
and Legends

OLD GRAVEYARDS and ghost stories go together, and New Jersey's cemeteries are no exception. Some of these stories have long been part of the state's folklore, others are local legends that I heard when I visited old burial grounds and talked with people about gravestones that caught my eye. The accounts in Part II include tales connected with those sites. But there are many other fascinating New Jersey graveyard legends about ghosts, mysterious deaths, and buried treasure that deserve to be retold. Here's a sampling to entice you into collecting stories yourself.

The Gravestone in the Parking Lot

In the most unromantic and unlikely of places—the parking lot of the Route 1 Flea Market—stands the gravemarker recording the tragic death of Mary Ellis. Back in the 1790s, Mary Ellis came to New Brunswick to stay with her younger sister, Margaret, and her husband, Colonel Anthony White. Records tell us that they bought a house on what is now Livingston Avenue at the present location of the George Street Playhouse. Mary met and fell in love with a sea captain, a former Revolutionary War officer whose name has never been identified. One day, her beloved captain, promising to return to Mary, sailed down the Raritan River to the Atlantic. He even left his horse for her to take care of while he was at sea. Each day, Mary went down to the banks of the Raritan, hoping for the first glimpse of her lover's return. The years rolled by, and still no sea captain. In 1813, Mary bought the piece of farmland along the river where she kept her daily watch. There she lived until her death in 1827, hopeful until the end that her captain would return to her.

21. The graves of Mary Ellis (d. 1827), family members, and possibly a horse in a private plot surrounded by an ornate wrought-iron fence. Photograph taken early twentieth century. (Courtesy Isaac J. Van Derveer Photograph Collection, Special Collections and Archives, Rutgers University Libraries.)

22. The Ellis plot in 1992, surrounded by a chain-link fence in the parking lot of the Route 1 Flea Market, New Brunswick.

Mary was buried on her plot of land; so was her sister Margaret, members of her niece's family, and—so legend has it—the sea captain's horse. The property was owned by the Evans family until the twentieth century; then it changed hands many times. At one time, it was even owned by one of the founders of Johnson & Johnson Pharmaceuticals.

In the early 1900s, the family burial plot was surrounded by an ornate wrought iron fence, in the midst of woods.

Today that peaceful setting is gone. In the 1960s the trees were cut down, the land was sold, and a parking lot was put in to serve the customers of a discount store. For security reasons, a chain-link fence has replaced the wrought-iron fence; the original gravemarkers are gone. A restriction on the land gives the heirs the right to enter the property to tend the graves or even to remove the remains, if all the descendants could agree to reinterment. But there are supposedly over a hundred descendants and they have no interest in changing the site. So there Mary Ellis rests, amid the bustle of the flea market, her final request honored over 160 years later.

Buried with Her Jewels

In the indolent village of Sykesville near McGuire Air Force Base in Burlington County are buried the remains of a woman who defied the maxim: "You can't take it with you." Emily Newbold Black died at age seventy-eight in 1899 and she did, indeed, take "it" with her. Before she died, she requested to be buried with her very beautiful and rare jewels. After she died, and her request was fulfilled, the church had to have watchmen guard the plot nightly to keep away greedy grave robbers. Today, behind the Plattsburgh Presbyterian Church lies a small burial plot for members of the Newbold and Black families. Emily's white sandstone marker and several others, obscured by weeds, vines, and shrubs, stand inside a wrought-iron enclosure. As far as anyone knows, the jewels are still with her.

Pirate Treasures

Blackbeard the Pirate spent much time in New Jersey's seaport towns and off our coast. Despite his mean character and unsavory appearance, he managed, it is said, to persuade twelve women to marry him—perhaps because he lavished his plunder on them. In 1717, returning from the high seas one dark and stormy night with a load of treasure, Blackbeard landed in the town of Burlington. He ordered his crew to dig a hole and bury the loot under a black walnut tree on Wood Street.

When a pirate volunteered to "guard" the treasure, Blackbeard shot

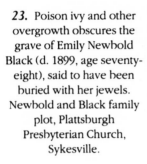

23. Poison ivy and other overgrowth obscures the grave of Emily Newbold Black (d. 1899, age seventy-eight), said to have been buried with her jewels. Newbold and Black family plot, Plattsburgh Presbyterian Church, Sykesville.

him in cold blood. Then he had the dead man buried upright, along with a small black dog. To this day, they say that on a stormy night in Burlington, the ghost of the little black dog can be seen near the old tree on Wood Street. No one has ever found the treasure.

Nor has anyone found the treasure of an earlier pirate, William Leeds, a member of Captain Kidd's crew in the 1600s. William Leeds gave up his piratical life and joined the Christ Episcopal Church in Shrewsbury, where he is buried in the cemetery near the north church tower. Leeds's gift of his ill-gotten pirate gold to the Episcopal churches of Middletown and Shrewsbury gave them a good income for years. Leeds left all of his possessions to the Shrewsbury church, including a sea chest with a hidden compartment. When the compartment was opened, there was nothing to be found, and since then, people have searched for William Leeds's treasure.

The Unsolved Deaths at Catawba Creek

Five mysterious deaths occurred at the West Mansion in Catawba Creek, near Great Egg Harbor, between May 1826 and September 1829. Four of the Wests died in the final three weeks of that period. The tombstones of the West parents and three children read as follows:

Thomas Biddle West, age 14, died after "50 hours illness,"
May 17, 1826
James West, age 19, died August 24, 1829
George West, Jr., age 23, died September 3, 1829
George West, Sr., age 53, died September 10, 1829
Amy West, September 15, 1829

The only surviving member of the family was Joe West, an attorney in Atlantic County. It was said that he had a very small law practice. But after the deaths of everyone else in his family, he moved into the mansion and lived in high style. Many suspected he had murdered them all, but the charge was never proven. Then one day Joe West disappeared, never to be heard of again.

The Ghosts of Ringwood Manor

Legends of ghosts haunting the estate of beautiful Ringwood Manor go back three centuries. The burial ground there may be the oldest in New Jersey. It was originally the final resting place of American Indians, then of miners who came from Germany and Ireland to work the iron mines in the 1700s (more than a dozen mines, now abandoned, lie within a mile of the house), and of the owners of Ringwood Manor. Many residents and visitors to the manor house have reported strange noises, the smells of cigars and cooking food, and the sight of people haunting about the house.

The nearby iron and copper mines had their own ghosts and frightening noises. The miners would run from the mines in terror, claiming that the moans and knockings portended an accident.

At "Sallie's Pond" behind the Manor, the ghost of a member of the Hewitt family, which owned the manor for many years, likes to scare away visitors. Early in the twentieth century, Sarah, or Sallie, Hewitt won local fame for her habit of driving—on horseback, even as an elderly woman—trespassers off the manor grounds. Now on some evenings her ghost rises above the surface of the waters, floating closer and closer to people fishing innocently at the pond. Tackle boxes and poles have been known to disappear.

The nineteenth-century Hewitts had their own ghost to contend with: that of Robert Erskine, a Scottish engineer who was the Ringwood mines' surveyor and manager during the late eighteenth century. Washington called on his services as a mapmaker during the Revolutionary War. On a military mapping expedition in 1780, Erskine, only forty-eight years old, died of pneumonia. He was laid to rest in a crypt at Ringwood Manor (see fig. 39). There, in the early nineteenth century, his ghost was seen for years, sitting on top of the crypt and holding a blue lantern. When the manor's owner, Mrs. Hewitt, finally repaired the crypt and replaced the bricks in its foundation, the ghost vanished at last, to everyone's relief.

The White Pilgrim and Other Warnings to Sinners

In 1835 a dramatic figure, dressed all in white, from white hat down to white boots, and riding on a white horse, traveled from village to village in northwestern New Jersey and Pennsylvania. Joseph Thomas, an itinerant preacher from Ohio, became known as the White Pilgrim. He came to Johnsonburg and preached a sermon to a crowd at the Episcopal Church. But before he could preach again, he died suddenly of smallpox. He was only forty-four.

Out of fear of contagion, he was buried at the Dark Moon Inn in a private burying ground maintained for criminals. Twelve years later, officials decided that Thomas could not infect the dead after all and allowed his body to be dug up and reinterred in the Johnsonburg Christian Church Cemetery. A large white monument dedicated to the White Pilgrim still stands in the burial ground.

Another notable preacher lies buried in the graveyard of the First United Methodist Church in Salem, New Jersey. Until he was thirty-three, Benjamin Abbott led a riotous life of drinking, fighting, and gambling. Then a series of visions and fainting spells came over him. He was tormented with dreams of scorpions, of evil spirits, of devils pulling him down to hell. The sinner turned to religion, reformed his wicked ways, and founded the first Methodist Society in New Jersey. Despite his lack of education and formal religious training, Abbott became a charismatic preacher. At the revival meetings he held around South Jersey, Pennsylvania, and Maryland, his simple language and emotional fervor had his listeners fall down fainting before him, recover miraculously from illness, and enjoy sudden conversions. For twenty-three years Reverend Abbott preached in and around Salem. He died of fever and ague (malaria) after preaching in Quintons Bridge in 1796. A plaque placed next to his gravestone by the Methodist Society honors this ordinary man whose extraordinary powers influenced so many people in the early days of the United States.

A gravestone in Edison, behind St. James Episcopal Church, marks the grave of an avowed atheist whose death preached as powerful a lesson as any that Abbott or the White Pilgrim ever gave. In 1835, Thomas W. Harper was in a tavern proudly celebrating the deed to his new house, the only brick house in all Piscatawaytown, when a tornado struck. Harper ran out and defied God to kill him. Right after he spoke these words, the high winds blew off the roof of the nearby church and a flying timber killed him on the spot. The story converted many an unbeliever in that neck of the woods. Harper's story and grave inscription (now illegible) were recorded by an antiquarian:

> Thomas W. Harper, a native of Bishopgate, London, England, who died June 23, 1835, aged 65 years. His death was caused by the falling of the English church during the great storm which occurred here in June 19th, 1835.
>
>
>
> Tired with wandering through a world of sin,
> Hither we come to nature's common inn
> To rest our wearied bodies for a night
> In hopes to rise in nature's truest light.
> This world's a city full of crooked streets
> And death a market-place where all men meet.
>
>

Part Two

A Guide to Notable New Jersey Burial Grounds

When You Visit
an Old Burial Ground

THIS GUIDE describes 127 old burial grounds in the twenty-one counties of
northern, central, and southern New Jersey—a mere handful of the thousands of graveyards in the state. One cemetery in each county is discussed
at length, and at least three others are noted more briefly. The three regional maps will help you find interesting cemeteries wherever you go in
the state. The numbers on the maps and their county-by-county keys cor-
respond to the entries in the guide. Each entry for a burial ground gives its
name and location and includes information about the people buried
there, about the gravemarkers and epitaphs, and about the cemetery's history and appearance. For the longer entries, I've given detailed directions
and suggestions for planning your visit.

Please follow common sense and good manners whenever you visit
a graveyard. Show your respect to the dead and to the customs of the
community by talking quietly and staying off the gravemounds. Treat the
grounds as you would a state park: do not disturb animals or pick plants
(clearing away overgrowth may actually damage the graves or markers).

Make sure that your visit is welcomed by the owner or caretaker.
Most cemeteries in New Jersey are accessible to the public (all the burial
grounds described in this guide are), but they may have designated visiting hours. Some have locked gates and require special permission. This is
especially true in crowded cities where cemeteries have been vandalized
or used as a hangout. Isolated rural cemeteries may not be locked, but are
also subject to vandalism. Unless you are a descendant of someone buried
in a private ground, you have no legal right to cross private property to
visit a grave or burial ground, no matter how innocent your intentions.
Many landowners will readily grant you permission, but you need to ask.

In any case, it is not a good idea to visit burial grounds alone. Ask a friend to join you.

The best time of year to visit an overgrown graveyard is winter or spring. Then you will be able to walk through the grounds without tripping on vines and shrubs. Winter snow and rain clean off the stones and make them easier to read. In summer and fall, be sure to take sunscreen, sun hat, sunglasses, and insect repellent. Watch out for poison ivy! I've gotten poison ivy twice, both times from casually brushing aside vines to read inscriptions. Gloves would have helped. The kind of underbrush that takes over all cemeteries is just the kind of habitat favored by the tick that carries Lyme disease. No matter what the season or what part of the state, assume that you are at risk of being bitten and protect yourself by wearing long sleeves, long pants tucked into your socks, and using an insect repellent. When you get home, take a shower and check carefully for the tiny ticks.

I have found it helpful to take along a notebook and pencil, a spray bottle, a soft rag or brush, and a 35mm camera stocked with *black-and-white* film with a 125 ASA rating. The cemetery inventory and gravestone forms in Appendixes 3 and 4 will remind you of information worth noting down. It's a good idea to sketch a plan of the cemetery in your notebook and mark the locations of stones that are of particular interest to you. To read inscriptions on stones obscured by dirt and bird droppings (New Jersey is a fabulous state for bird watching, and birds find safe refuge in many graveyards), use the spray bottle and rag to wipe the stones gently. If the droppings don't come off, don't scrub—you might erode the stone.

For good, sharp pictures of gravestones, take a photograph when the sun is directly on the face of the tombstone, with no shadows. Some gravestone photographers take a large door mirror and reflect the sun onto the face of the stone—a very effective but strenuous technique. A yellow filter is also recommended for sharp pictures. For more detailed information, consult the excellent book *Early Gravestone Art,* by Francis Y. Duval and Ivan B. Rigby.

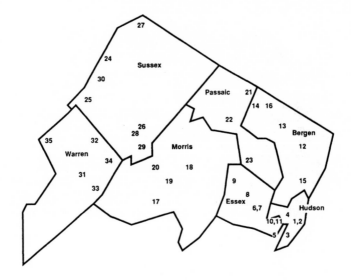

Northern New Jersey

Hudson County

1 Jersey City—Old Bergen Church Burial Ground
2 Jersey City—Speer Burial Ground
3 Jersey City—Bayview Cemetery
4 Kearney—Arlington Cemetery

Essex County

5 Hillside—Evergreen Cemetery
6 Belleville—Christ Episcopal Churchyard
7 Belleville—Dutch Reformed Church Cemetery
8 Bloomfield—First Presbyterian Church Cemetery
9 Fairfield—Fairfield Reformed Church Burial Ground
10 Newark—Mount Pleasant Cemetery
11 Newark—Old First Church Cemetery

Bergen County

12 Hackensack—Reformed Dutch Churchyard
13 Ridgewood—Old Paramus Reformed Church Burial Ground
14 Mahwah—Moffat Road Lutheran Cemetery
15 Little Ferry—Gethsemane African-American Cemetery
16 Mahwah—Ramapo Reformed Church Burial Ground

Morris County

17 Mendham—Hilltop Presbyterian Church Burial Ground
18 Whippany—Whippany Burial Ground
19 Morristown—Presbyterian Churchyard
20 Randolph—Dover Quaker Meetinghouse Burial Ground

Passaic County

21 Ringwood—Ringwood Manor Burial Ground
22 Wanaque—Wanaque Burial Ground
23 Wayne—Preakness Reformed Dutch Cemetery

Sussex County

24 Bevans—Bevans/Peters Valley Cemetery
25 Flatbrookville—Old Dutch Reformed Cemetery
26 Lafayette—Lafayette Cemetery
27 Montague—Minisink Burial Ground
28 Newton—Old Newton Burial Ground
29 Sparta—Sparta Cemetery
30 Walpack Center—Walpack Burial Ground

Warren County

31 Hope—Moravian Burial Ground
32 Yellow Frame—Yellow Frame Presbyterian Church Cemetery
33 Hackettstown—Hackettstown Presbyterian Cemetery
34 Johnsonburg—Old Christian Church Cemetery
35 Pahaquarry—Calno Burial Ground

Northern New Jersey

Hudson County

1   *Old Bergen Church Burial Ground*
Jersey City
1600s

Directions: Take Exit 14C from the New Jersey Turnpike, and follow signs to the Grand Street exit. Take Grand Street exit and stay in left lane while leaving exit ramp. Turn left at the traffic light onto Montgomery Street. From Montgomery Street, continue on for about ten blocks to the intersection with Bergen Avenue. Turn right onto Bergen, go two blocks, and the church will be on your left, the burial grounds opposite and on the right.

The Old Bergen Church Burial Ground occupies several acres in a parklike setting within highly urbanized Jersey City. This burial ground is noteworthy because it contains gravemarkers of many prominent early Dutch families who settled here in the 1600s. These families were affiliated with the Old Bergen Church, the oldest organized congregation west of the Hudson River. The large white church dates from 1841 and is the third church to be built on this site. The earlier two were not large enough to accommodate the growing congregation. In building the present structure, old bricks were re-used, and then covered with stucco. The church's charter, on display in the church, was signed in 1660 by the mayor of the Dutch town of Wagening. Gerit Gerritsen and his wife, who are named in the charter as religious representatives, and the Gerritsens' descendants from then on became known as "Van Wagenen," i.e., from Wagening, with various spellings. Some of the Wagenen family descendants are buried in Old Bergen burial grounds.

The burial ground contains about 150 tombstones on a small hill surrounded by a concrete retaining wall and iron fence. The wall prevents further erosion of the hill. The gate in the middle of the iron fence is kept locked to keep out trespassers. If you stand outside the gate, you will not see much, because the fronts of the tombstones face east, away from Bergen Avenue, in keeping with an old burial ground custom.

Old Bergen Church has taken an active role in maintaining the burial grounds over the years, and the immediate area is very well-lit at night and on a main thoroughfare, so vandalism has not been a serious problem.

Begin your tour by walking through the gate and up the steps, passing by the two Tise family marble markers, right at the top of the steps. These date from the mid-1800s and contain interesting epitaphs. Both tombstones have had cracks repaired over the years and are in fair condition. From here, walk to the right, under the shady oak trees to the Van Wagenen granite monument. The letters on the bottom of the tall monument can be easily read and are one of the few inscriptions that face Bergen Street. This area is the Wagenen family plot and spans several generations. One of the older Wagenen gravemarkers, made from brown sandstone, reads:

> In Memory of Leah
> daughter of John Van Wagenen,
> and Wife of
> Henry Brinkerhoff
> who departed this life
> the 7th day of July
> 1824 aged 68 years
> 8 months and 24 days
> To this world have bid adieu
> Soon will be the turn for you
> Remember me whilst in your mind
> Be a friend to all mankind

Walking toward the center of the grounds, away from the Wagenen markers, you will find tombstones for the Van Winkle family dating from the early 1800s. It is no coincidence that Washington Irving used this name in his wonderful story about Rip Van Winkle, the Dutchman who wandered in the Catskill Mountains of New York and fell asleep for twenty

24. The gravemarkers of Martin and Abraham Tise, facing east in anticipation of Judgment Day. Cracks in the gravestones have been repaired, and the cemetery is well maintained, but litter dropped by passers-by continues to be a nuisance. Old Bergen Church Burial Ground, Jersey City.

years: Irving was a frequent visitor to Bergen and was an acquaintance of the Van Winkle family. One Van Winkle brown sandstone marker reads:

> In Memory of
> Daniel Van Winkle
> who departed this life
> the 19th day of December
> 1823
> aged 8 years
> 10 months and 13 days

This brownstone marker is typical of the very simple design of many old markers in Old Bergen, rounded or urn-shaped on top with no imagery. Many have epitaphs, but not all of them can be read. Several of the names inscribed on the headstones can also be found on street signs in Jersey City: Van Wagenen, Van Winckle, Van Houten, Van Vorst, Newkirk, Brinkerhoff, and Merseles. As you continue walking through the burial grounds, read the epitaphs. I liked the poem on a sandstone marker near the Van Winkle stones:

> This stone is erected In Memory of William Needham
> who died February 27th 1807 aged 70 years 6 months and 10 days
> Fearless and calm he met the final blow
> And left without a sigh these scenes below
> A band of cherubs join'd him on the road
> And safe convey'd him to the bright abode
> Where perfect spirits sweet communion hold
> And chaunt seraphic airs to harps of gold

Be sure to visit the section of the burial ground in the back that borders Tuers Avenue. Notice the square granite blocks and a few surviving iron rails that originally marked off square plots. This part of the burial ground is not as well maintained; some tombstones have been toppled over or have sunk low into the ground amid the tall grass and weeds. Watch out for the poison ivy. All the way in the back, on a hill overlooking Tuers Avenue, a monument honors Reverend John Cornelison, who was minister of Old Bergen Church from 1806 to 1828.

Around the corner from the Old Bergen Burial Grounds is Speer Cemetery, also worth a visit. The surrounding area once comprised the borderline of the fort of the original village of Bergen, which is said to have been one of the first permanent settlements in New Jersey. Today it is bordered by streets named after early settlers: Vroom, Van Reypen, Newkirk, and Tuers. Also notable is the Dutch architectural style of some of the older buildings in the area.

Planning your visit: The burial ground is kept locked, so call the Old Bergen Church to arrange a visit (201-433-1815). You can find metered parking on Bergen Avenue right next to the burial grounds, or look for parking on the side streets. The area is on a bus route and within five blocks of the train station at Journal Square. The burial ground is several steps up from street level and is mostly grass covered. The area has its share of home-lessness, crime and other urban problems, so keep your camera, purse, and other personal belongings secure. During one of my visits, I witnessed a purse-snatching incident directly in front of the cemetery entrance! Watch out too for the pack of dogs kept fenced in an adjacent backyard. Occasionally the dogs escape and chase visitors to the burial grounds.

2 ?? *Speer Burial Ground*
   Jersey City
   1600s

Directions: Take Exit 14C from the New Jersey Turnpike, and follow signs to the Grand Street exit. Take Grand Street exit and stay in left lane while leaving exit ramp. Turn left at the traffic light onto Montgomery Street. From Montgomery Street, continue on for about ten blocks to the intersection with Bergen Avenue. Turn right onto Bergen, go three blocks, and just past the Old Bergen Church turn left onto Vroom Street to the cemetery on your immediate left.

Speer Burial Ground, dating from the 1660s, is said to be the oldest ceme-tery of European settlers in New Jersey. Today it is in one of the most congested urban areas of the state, just blocks away from Journal Square. Occupying a little over an acre, this L-shaped burial ground hides behind tall brick buildings whose store-front facades line Bergen Avenue. In 1661, Peter Stuyvesant, the governor of the Dutch West India Company, granted a charter for the earliest known European settlement in New Jersey: the village of Bergen. The DeMotts, a family of early Dutch colonists who dared to settle west of the Hudson, in this wild and beautiful hilly area inhabited by Indians and a handful of other Dutch families, used part of this land for a family burial plot. In 1857, a section of the DeMott estate was purchased by Abraham Speer, a Jersey City mortician. He began sell-ing burial plots at sixteen dollars a piece, and the tract became known as Speer Burial Ground.

Expect strong emotions when you visit Speer: there are good rea-sons for it to be referred to as "The Forgotten Cemetery." Back in the 1960s and 1970s, the cemetery was unfenced and totally neglected. Unfortu-nately, local teens used it for a hangout and for partying. Markers were stolen or broken, spray-painted, and marred with graffiti. In the 1970s, concerned citizens were able to get Public Service Gas & Electric to donate a street light to keep the area illuminated at night for police patrols. At the same time, a chain-link fence was erected to keep vandals out. Now there is even a locked gate on Vroom Avenue. The gate has not deterred vandals, who continue a long, unpleasant tradition: even in the early 1900s, city dwellers were complaining about the disgraceful conditions to be found at Speer. Plans were then made to make the site more attractive. Over the years, cleanup crews have come in to clean up, and groups of people have volunteered their time to mow and pick up litter. Recently, even prisoners were put to the task. But no one group has consistently taken responsibility for the upkeep or restoration of Speer. In 1984, the city planners had ambitious plans to landscape the area, put in walkways and benches, and repair the headstones, similar to what was done at the Old Trinity Churchyard in Manhattan. The plans were never implemented. In fact, this historic area came very close to being turned into a multi-level parking garage by the Jersey City Parking Authority in the late 1960s. The plan was abandoned when the American Legion and a citizens' group opposed it.

Restoration of the Speer Burial Ground would be difficult. No one is even certain how many people are buried there, since a complete list of burial names has never been found. No map exists to assure us that the stones still stand where the burials took place. It is likely that stones have been moved during various cleanups and acts of vandalism. The best guess is that several hundred persons were buried at Speer, with about 160 gravemarkers made from sandstone, marble, and granite. Speer is known to have been used as a potter's field in the 1800s; some estimate thousands of paupers may have been buried there without markers or records.

The number of underground vaults is also uncertain. The outline of the DeMott family brick vault is very clear on the ground, but today, only a small portion of the vault can be seen above ground. The DeMott family tombstone is nearby. The earliest remaining gravemarker at Speer is dated 1756, although it is believed that the grounds were used even earlier. The last burials were completed after World War I. Many veterans of the Revolutionary War, Civil War, War of 1812, Spanish-American War, and even World War I were buried here.

As in the Old Bergen Church Burial Ground and Bayview Cemetery, many burials at Speer took place in family plots sectioned off by granite

25. The underground vault of the DeMott family, Speer Burial Ground, Jersey City. The number and identities of the dead buried here are not known. Empty liquor bottles surround the entrance, and paper sacks litter the vault opening.

blocks marking the four corners. One of these plots belongs to an early Dutch family named Terhune, and its markers are near the front gate of Speer. Stephen Terhune's white marble marker is embedded horizontally on a hill near the taller Terhune monument. His tombstone is broken in half, with vegetation growing all around it, partially obscuring the inscription:

> In Memory of Stephen Terhune
> who died Dec 20th 1865
> Dearest husband thou hast left me
> Here thy loss I deeply feel
> But my God that hath bereft me
> He may will my soul to heal

On the opposite side of the Terhune monument near a fence is the grave of three members of the Jann Family. Its white sandstone marker doesn't resemble other markers in the area, with its attractive fanlike design on top, the phrase "Here rests in God" underneath, and the delicately

26. The marble marker for Stephen Terhune (d. 1865) cracked in half and covered with ivy, with a beautiful tribute from his wife. Speer Burial Ground, Jersey City.

carved inscription. This unique gravemarker dates from 1865 and the stonecarver's identity is not known.

Scattered throughout the burial ground are gravemarkers of sandstone, granite, and marble ranging from poor to good condition. Many inscriptions cannot be read because tall weeds and vines (including poison ivy throughout the grounds) cover the writing. A plaque at the front of the burial ground declares that the site was restored by the city of Jersey City and rededicated on Memorial Day, 1979. It is obvious that a total restoration was never completed. Hope remains that funds will be found to improve this forgotten burial ground of Jersey City's earliest unknown citizens and soldiers.

Planning your visit: Because the burial ground is kept locked, you need to contact the Hudson County Division of Cultural and Heritage Affairs at (201) 915-1212 to arrange for a visit.

27. An unusually designed and inscribed marker for members of the Jann family, near the entrance, Speer Burial Ground, Jersey City. The shadows from the tree branches made me think of two arms reaching down to the stone.

If you park at the meters near the Old Bergen Church, you may be able to see both burial grounds at the same time, as they are just around the corner from each other. They are within five blocks of the train station at Journal Square and on the bus route. The warnings for Old Bergen Church Burial Ground apply here too: this is a high crime area.

Other Notable Burial Grounds in Hudson County

3 ☙ Bayview Cemetery, along Garfield Avenue, Jersey City.
Open to the public, this cemetery is in a parklike setting with thousands
of burials: mausoleums, monuments, and ordinary markers from the nineteenth and twentieth centuries. The burial plots are organized by numbers.
At the bottom of the hill is the Cunard Plot, which has a wonderful view
of the New York skyline. A monument honors "dead shipmates"—more
than thirty men who died while in service for Cunard Steamship Lines.
Only fourteen of them are actually buried here; the rest were lost at sea.

4 ☙ Arlington Cemetery, Schuyler Avenue and Belleville Pike, Kearney.
There are thousands of graves of former settlers of Hudson County, a few
dating back to the 1800s. Kearney was settled by many Scots, so a large
number of the markers will contain Scottish names. Arlington also contains the markers and remains from a section of Old Bergen Cemetery in
Jersey City. The bodies were exhumed when a road was widened early in
the twentieth century.

Essex County

5   ☙ *Evergreen Cemetery*
         Hillside
         1800s

Directions: From the Garden State Parkway, take Exit 140 to Route 22 east. Continue driving through Hillside; just past the Auto Mall, look for the Hillside Avenue
exit. Turn right onto Hillside Avenue and continue a short distance to North Broad
Street. Make another right onto North Broad Street. The cemetery is a short way up
North Broad Street on your left.

This 115-acre burial ground is actually in two counties, Essex and Union.
Many notable Americans are buried here. The site is listed in the National
Register of Historic Places. The cemetery, like many established during
the Victorian era, has a parklike setting with beautiful landscaping. Birdwatchers and naturalists have sighted fox, deer, woodchucks, and a great

variety of birds. In the 1800s, goats were allowed to roam free in the cemetery to keep the grass short. The cemetery has a truly quiet, rural feel to it even though it is surrounded by city. Bustling Newark Airport is only a mile away.

The approximately five thousand tombstones, mausoleums, and statues are made mainly of marble, although there are some wooden crosses as well. The variety of gravemarker styles to be found here is striking. Look for typically Victorian motifs like the willow and urn, flowers, and trees. If you look closely, you can find photos attached to many gravestones. These protected photos have worn well over the years.

Evergreen Cemetery has several interesting special sections. A walk through a group of graves of orphaned children who died from diphtheria in the nineteenth century underscores the devastation of this terrible disease before immunization eradicated it in the twentieth century. A section of graves of Gypsies has ornate monuments in unusual styles. This section was used as a site for the film *King of the Gypsies*.

Two Jewish cemeteries make up subsections of Evergreen: Oheb Sholem and Bnai Jeshuron. Many of the tombstones contain Hebrew lettering and dates, and Jewish stars.

Evergreen Cemetery is well known for its graves of famous writers, buried throughout the cemetery in their respective family plots. Mary Mapes Dodge, author of *Hans Brinker, or the Silver Skates,* which was translated into six languages, was buried here in 1905. She grew up in Newark but lived in New York City with her husband and two sons. Left a widow at age twenty-seven, she returned to her father's home in Newark and began her literary career there. She launched a magazine in 1873 and became a leader in writing juvenile literature. The writer Stephen Crane was born in Newark in 1871, the son of a Methodist minister. He achieved some notoriety for writing his first novel, *Maggie: A Girl of the Streets,* in 1892. It was a very controversial book for the times, as it told the story of a young woman driven to suicide by sweatshop labor practices and a life of poverty. Crane's second and better-known novel was *The Red Badge of Courage,* the story of a soldier during the Civil War who had some tough decisions to make. Crane died of tuberculosis in England in 1900, at the young age of twenty-eight. Another novelist whose books were widely read is Edward Stratemeyer, who used pen names when writing the Bobbsey Twins series, *Tom Swift,* and *The Rover Boys*. He lived in nearby Elizabeth, died in 1930 at age sixty-eight, and is now buried in a family plot at Evergreen.

Scattered throughout this burial ground are many markers that identify soldiers' graves. Some of these tombstones display VFW emblems that indicate a soldier's rank during various overseas wars. A separate section is devoted to Civil War graves, and a cannon used in the war decorates the grounds.

Four former government leaders were also buried here: State Senator John Kean and three members of the House of Representatives.

Evergreen Cemetery is still in use and attracts visitors from many ethnic groups. The various customs observed by these groups are much apparent during one's visit to this lovely parklike setting.

Planning your visit: The cemetery is surrounded by a fence. There are designated visiting hours, and the gates are open between the hours of 8 A.M. and 4:45 P.M. A security guard is on the premises during visiting hours. Stop at the building near the main entrance for a map, as you will need assistance in finding the more notable burial locations. For further information, call (908) 352-7940.

Other Notable Burial Grounds in Essex County

6 ❧ *Christ Episcopal Churchyard,* Main and William Streets, Belleville.
A narrow driveway next to the church leads back to a lovely burial ground in a parklike setting. Recent landscaping efforts have resulted in walkways and various shrub plantings that make this a very attractive place. Some of the older tombstones from the 1700s are in fragile condition, and no stone rubbing is allowed. Especially notable is the flat tombstone of Sarah Frances Smith, decorated with angel effigies in each corner.

7 ❧ *Dutch Reformed Church Cemetery,* Main and Rutgers Streets,
    Belleville.
Behind this brown sandstone church built in 1725 is a burial ground containing the remains of sixty Revolutionary War veterans. Their names are inscribed on a plaque on the front of the church, placed there by the Daughters of the American Revolution. Here also is the gravemarker of Henry Rutgers, for whom Rutgers University is named. Other gravemarkers identify men who were killed in the Belleville Powder Mill Explo-

28. The very attractive marker for Thomas Tyson (d. 1795, age sixty-eight), Christ Episcopal Churchyard, Belleville. The marker was probably carved by Uzal Ward of Newark. Compare this headstone to the one from Mount Pleasant Cemetery, Newark, shown in figure 30.

sion on April 20, 1814. Josiah Hornblower, pioneer and engineer, is also buried here. The burial ground is in rough shape: tombstones are toppled and broken and the grounds need some work.

**8 ** *First Presbyterian Church Cemetery,* Broad Street and Belleville Avenue, Bloomfield.
Within the Bloomfield Green Historic Area stands this sandstone church, dating back to 1797. Behind the church are hundreds of red sandstone markers with interesting epitaphs from the 1700s.

**9 ** *Fairfield Reformed Church Burial Ground,* Main Street, Fairfield.
Here is an early Dutch burial ground from the late 1700s. It is noted for its excellent examples of rhyming epitaphs inscribed on several hundred sandstone markers. Be sure to read the one about "the bones of Thomas Speer," who died in 1829.

29. Elongated angel effigy on sandstone tombstone of Elizabeth Speer (d. 1791). Dutch Reformed Church Cemetery, Belleville. The church, built in 1725, has walls made of native sandstone.

30. An angel effigy sandstone marker for Jemime Canfield (d. 1793, age forty-two), Mount Pleasant Cemetery, Newark. The style is the same as found in Christ Episcopal Churchyard, Belleville, and was probably carved by Uzal Ward of Newark (see fig. 28).

31. Two of the few surviving seventeenth-century gravemarkers in New Jersey: Ellena Johnson (d. November 2, 1694) and her husband, Thomas (who died three days later). Mount Pleasant Cemetery, Newark.

10 ❧ *Mount Pleasant Cemetery,* on Broadway near the New Jersey
        Historical Society, Newark.

This burial ground is now listed on the National Register of Historic Places.
Mount Pleasant is comprised of thirty-six acres of mainly Victorian tombstones from the 1800s. Even older sandstone markers are also scattered
throughout, some dating back to 1694.

11 ❧ *Old First Church Cemetery,* on Broad near Market Street, down-
        town Newark.

Park on Edison Place to view this cemetery, dating from 1719. The church
was first a Puritan congregation, then a Presbyterian one, and contains
graves from the 1700s of Newark's earliest citizens.

Bergen County

12 ❧ *Reformed Dutch Churchyard*
         Hackensack
         1696

Directions: Take Exit 18 from the New Jersey Turnpike, and proceed to Route 46
west into Hackensack. After crossing over the Hackensack River Bridge, turn right
onto the Bergen Turnpike. Drive about two miles and look for the large white neo-
classic courthouse. Slow down and look for Court Street on your left. Turn left onto
Court Street. The burial grounds and church are two blocks up on your right. The
Village Green and Bergen County Courthouse are adjacent to the church and burial
grounds. Parking is limited: try the Village Green or the municipal lot nearby.

The thirty-three original communicants of this early Dutch congregation
would be greatly surprised to revisit the present site of their church and
burial ground. The location, once surrounded by woods, is now in the
middle of downtown Hackensack. The adjacent Village Green, where
townspeople gathered centuries ago to exchange news and hold social
events, is still there. Now office workers can be seen eating their lunch
or relaxing while sitting on the benches set up in the Green. Statues
of Brigadier General Enoch Poor, a Revolutionary War hero, and of an
American soldier look down on the Green. Across the street, surrounded
by a tall wrought-iron fence, are the church and burial ground. On a sunny

32. Bricks inscribed with the names of the founders of the congregation can be found at the front doorway of "the Church on the Green" (Reformed Dutch Churchyard) in Hackensack. Members of Peter Zabrisky's family are buried in the cemetery.

day, one can see the bright copper rooster, brought over from Holland in 1691, gleaming on top of the church steeple. Note the architecture of the church, for it is one of the oldest New Jersey churches. Originally built in 1696, the church has been rebuilt and enlarged twice. Many bricks are from the original building, and some even have the founders' names carved on them; they can still be seen clearly around the front doorway, some three hundred years later! The brick for the original founder reads: "Reverend Guilaem Bertholf BG ANNO 1696." The members of some founder families are buried in the churchyard, including families named Varick, Housman, Terhune, Ciesner, Brinkerhoff, Romeyn, and Zabrisky.

Walk through the gate in front of the church out to the burial ground, and note some of the older sandstone markers that are positioned around the walls of the church. The markers were placed there after church additions were made right on top of the graves. These markers date from the late 1700s and early 1800s and are made from red and brown sandstone. Some are decorated with death's head effigies common at that time. One of the brown sandstone markers near the back steps of the church contains this epitaph:

In
memory of
Mary Young
Wife of William Young
who departed this life
January 23rd 1811
Aged 75 Years
A tender wife,
A parent dear:
A pious mind,
And friend sincere.

The best known tombstone is that of Brigadier General Enoch Poor, a Revolutionary War commander from New Hampshire who died September 8, 1780, at age forty-four. Washington, Lafayette, and soldiers from the

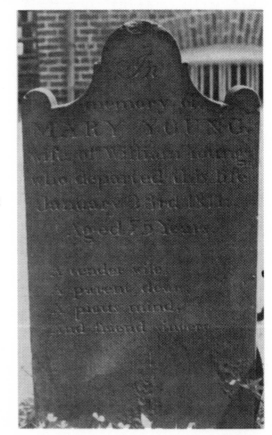

33. The sandstone gravemarker of Mary Young (d. 1811, age seventy-five), Reformed Dutch Churchyard, Hackensack.

American army attended General Poor's funeral and burial at this site in 1780. Enoch Poor's gravesite is located close to the corner nearest the Bergen County Courthouse and Commons. Nearby is the marker of Peter Wilson, a well-known Scotsman of the time and professor of languages at Columbia College, who died August 1, 1825, at age seventy-nine. Here also lie the remains of eighteen Revolutionary War soldiers, twenty-two Civil War veterans, and one veteran of the Mexican War. Walking toward the back of the church, note the large monument enclosed by an iron fence. Here are markers of the Varick family, early founders of the church. Richard Varick, former mayor of New York City, died July 30, 1851, at age seventy.

Several hundred gravemarkers in this burial ground date from the 1700s to early 1900s. Be sure to look for the early sandstone markers and fieldstones, some inscribed part in Dutch and part in English. The earliest marker is a simple fieldstone, curved at the top, with the initials "H B" on top and "1713" underneath; but it is unique because of the Indian symbols on it, said to represent the grave of a female Indian slave. A walk through this well-kept burial ground makes one aware of the importance of the Hackensack area in early American pioneer life, and of the diverse cultures that shaped colonial Bergen County.

Planning your visit: The burial ground is accessible through a latched, but not locked, gate. Parking is more readily available on weekends, right in the Commons area. The Commons is frequently the site of art and craft shows. It is generally a safe area, but on early mornings one can find the homeless sleeping in the burial grounds.

13 ❧ *Old Paramus Reformed Church Burial Ground*
   Ridgewood
   1735

Directions: From the Garden State Parkway, take Exit 166 to Route 17 north. The church and burial grounds are on the west side of the highway at 660 East Glen Avenue.

The entire area has been designated a National Landmark, because its first church, the Dutch Reformed, was used as a headquarters for Washington and the Continental Army during the Revolutionary War. At this site also, General Charleš Lee was court-martialed and dismissed for his retreat at the Battle of Monmouth. In 1782, Aaron Burr, vice president of the United States from 1801 to 1805, was married inside the church to Theodosia Provost.

The many tombstone markers that reflect the ethnic makeup of the settlers in the area make this burial ground a fascinating one to visit. Many tombstones dating before 1820 contain inscriptions written in Dutch, as the Dutch began settling here in 1666. The burial grounds behind the church consist of about 600 tombstones, including 125 fieldstones with no inscriptions. The burial grounds are also notable for their interesting epitaphs.

The following Dutch words will help you decipher many of the tombstones. *Geboren* means "born" and *overleden* or *gestorven* refers to "date of death." In Dutch culture, women usually kept their birth name upon marriage, or added their married name to their birth name. (Dutch women were also permitted to be property owners, a rare occurrence among other cultures in the 1700s.) Children's names appear mainly under their father's name, but sometimes the mother's name is inscribed first. In the older section close to the church are many old brown and red sandstone markers with Dutch words. For example, there are the Ackerman and Vander Beek stones, which are clustered together and contain fine examples of Dutch inscriptions. One such stone reads:

Van Der Beek Anno 1718
Den 17 Van Mey
Is Geboren poulis Van Der Beek
En Hy is Overleden
In Het Yaar 1795
Den 10 Maart

Here also is an example of a woman with both birth and married names given:

Ackerman
Stevens, Polly
wife of Abraham
d Feb 8, 1816
aged 22 years 11 months and 23 days

Several tombstones tell the story of an era when children did not always live into adulthood. This is evident in five tombstones in a far section of the yard marking the Carlock children's graves:

> Carlock, infant of Abraham and Maria, d. Aug. 21, 1840, aged 9 hours
> Carlock, son of Abraham and Maria, d. Aug. 7, 1839, aged 12 days
> Carlock, Rachael Catherine, daughter of Abraham and Maria, d. Oct. 29, 1837, aged 8 months and 3 days
> Carlock, Abraham, son of Abraham and Maria, d. Sept. 11, 1838, aged 5 months and 2 days
> Carlock, Jeremiah, son of Abraham and Maria, d. Sept. 2, 1839, aged 9 years, 1 month and 14 days

These five stones tell the tragedy of a couple who lost five children between the ages of 9 hours to 9 years. All deaths occurred between the years of 1837 and 1840. Interestingly, next to the last tombstone is another Carlock tombstone with the inscription:

> Carlock, Eleanor Lavinia, daughter of Jacob and Maria, d. March 12, 1844, aged 6 months.

This makes one wonder if this is the same Maria mentioned above. Did her husband Abraham die and she remarried? Where are the tombstones of Maria and Abraham? These are the kinds of questions one encounters during a walk through a burial ground. A genealogist may be able to find answers to such questions.

Some earlier tombstones, which pre-date the Revolutionary War period, are difficult to read. In the first row behind the church, a fieldstone marker located between other crude markers (look for a grouping of twelve in a row) appears to be inscribed "Ackerman, AN 1706, SAM." This is possibly the earliest dated stone on the grounds, though many may be from a similar time. Other markers in the same general area are from the 1760s but seem to have deteriorated since they were copied by a historian in 1931. Some of the other early settlers' names included here are Terhune, Conklin, Delamarter, Winters, Banta, Baldwin, Hopper, and Van Buskirk, among many others. This copy can be seen in the article about the Paramus Church Yard in volume 8 of the *New Jersey Genealogical Magazine*, pages 39–90.

34. A crudely inscribed small fieldstone marker in the Paramus Reformed Dutch Burial Ground, Ridgewood.

This beautiful old stone church and cemetery have become a landmark along busy Route 17, now near bustling shopping centers in suburban New Jersey. Vandalism is not a problem here, for the area is always well lit at night, with the tall steeple and gravestones reflecting the streetlights along the highway.

Planning your visit: The grounds are open to the public and there is ample parking in the church parking lot. The grounds are well maintained, so weeds and overgrowth are not a problem. For further information, contact the church at (201) 444-5933.

14 ❧ Moffat Road Lutheran Cemetery
Mahwah
1745

Directions: From the Garden State Parkway, take Exit 163 to Route 17 north. Moffat Road is about 10 miles north, off Route 17. (If traffic is heavy, you may want to turn right on Island Road instead.) Turn left onto Moffat Road to the burial grounds, on the corner of Moffat and Island Roads. The burial ground is on a hill overlooking Route 17.

Moffat Burial Ground has a startling location—a wooded hill about 30 feet high and within 50 feet of busy Route 17. Access to the grounds has become easier since the placement of a wooden staircase off Moffat Road. Large railroad ties hold the stairs in place and keep the hill of sand from constant erosion. A local Boy Scout troop has taken responsibility for building the wall along Moffat Road. The Mahwah Historic Preservation Commission is restoring the site, which contains about one hundred markers or fragments that had been neglected and vandalized. Work is not yet complete: several of the older stones are in the process of being restored by Lynette Strangstad, a graveyard preservationist from Charleston, South Carolina.

As a plaque informs visitors, the area was settled by German Palatine families in 1713. Around 1720, they built a log church near this site and obtained the land for a burial ground. The earliest dated marker is a simple stone marker inscribed "P B 1745." You can find it if you start at the top of the stairs and walk toward the right and to the back of the grounds; it

35. The gravemarker of Ellen Hemmion (d. 1814, age ninety-one), one of four simple Hemmion family gravemarkers. Moffat Road Lutheran Cemetery, Mahwah. This shows one of the finest letterings to be found on a fieldstone in the state.

is in front of the four Hemion family stones. Note that there are two different spellings for the family name: Hemion and Hemmion. Variant spellings
were common in early America, as spelling was not standardized. The
Ellen Hemmion marker is very nicely inscribed for such a crude stone
marker.

Once you have seen the Hemmion markers, walk back toward the
stairs and you will find the base of a sandstone marker. About two inches
of a stone signed by John Zuricher is visible here. Zuricher carved stones
for many burial grounds in the Hudson Valley area.

Nearby the Zuricher stone and next to the stairs is a serviceberry, or
shadbush, tree with many trunks. In pioneer days in the springtime, the
preacher could finally perform services such as marriages and baptisms
that often had to be postponed in the winter because of bad roads and
weather. This was about the same time the shadbush was in bloom, so the
tree came to be known as the "serviceberry."

Some of the names one comes across in the burial ground are
Wanamaker, Frederick, Bevans, Messenger, Falli, Ausband, and Fox. Many
of the stones are unmarked fieldstones, with no information about who
was buried under them. One marker was removed since the 1970s, when
the stones were transcribed, and no one knows what happened to it. It
was inscribed as follows:

> Here lyeth the body of John Suffern
> son of John and Mary Suffern of New Antrim
> was born the First day of February A.D. 1776.
> Departed this life the 15 of January 1777.
> Aged 11 months and 15 Days.

John's parents are buried in the nearby Reformed Church Cemetery.

What makes this cemetery interesting are the many markers carved
with the simple folk art of the early pioneers in this then-wild part of New
Jersey.

Planning your visit: The burial grounds are open to visitors. You are not
allowed to touch any of the more fragile markers, particularly those un-
dergoing restoration. The area is rather wooded and dark, so taking pictures may be difficult without a flash. Don't walk too close to the edge, as
you may inadvertently contribute to the continuous problem of erosion of
the hill.

Other Notable Burial Grounds in Bergen County

15 ❧ Gethsemane African-American Cemetery, Little Ferry.

This is a small, abandoned African-American burial ground with approximately fifty graves and markers. It was recently taken over by the Bergen County Division of Cultural and Historic Affairs with an eye to performing some restoration work and research. It is said to contain many graves of early slaves, as well as examples of folk-art fieldstones. Because he was denied burial in the all-white Hackensack Cemetery, the black sexton Samuel Bass was buried in 1884 in Gethsemane. The controversy over this prohibition led to the passage of the Negro Burial Bill, which disallowed race as a reason to deny burial in a specific cemetery.

16 ❧ Ramapo Reformed Church Burial Ground, West Ramapo Avenue and Island Road, off Route 17, Mahwah.

This burial ground dates from 1795 and contains several hundred stones of early Dutch and German settlers. The church and cemetery were jointly shared by the Lutherans and Dutch Reformed on alternating weeks until 1848, when the second church was built. A part of the cemetery that was used for African-American burials in the 1800s is in a separate area.

Morris County

17 ❧ Hilltop Presbyterian Church Burial Ground
Mendham
1749

Directions: From Interstate 287 in New Brunswick, take Exit 22 to Route 525 north. This will lead you right into the town of Mendham. From Main Street (Route 24) turn onto Hilltop Road to the church and burial grounds.

When approaching Mendham, you will see that the Hilltop Church is a landmark in the middle of the village. The church, built in 1860, is an example of a simple style that was actually popular earlier, during the eighteenth century. This is the fourth church to be built at this site, the first one

36. The double headstone for Phebe and Abraham Day, Hilltop Presbyterian
Church Burial Ground, Mendham. Abraham died thirty-eight years after his wife,
so the clasped hands may symbolize their reunion in the afterlife.

dating back to the 1700s. Amazingly, two of these earlier churches were
struck by lightning. In fact, on May 16, 1813, at the close of Sunday morning services, eight to ten people were struck by lightning that shot through
the window. One of them, Martha Drake, died and was buried under a
sycamore tree in the Thompson plot. The inscription on the red sandstone
marker has crumbled away, though the marker is still intact. According to
earlier accounts, the inscription read:

Martha, wife of John Drake
was killed instantly by
lightning as she sat
Church on Sunday the 16th of
May, 1813, aged 33 years, 6 months
and 24 days

How sudden, Oh how sudden was the stroke of death
That instantly all mortal ties dissolved
And left the lifeless corpse bereav'd of breath,
And friends and relatives in grief involved.
The pain of death and parting friends unknown,
She quickly passed the bounds of mortal life;
The immortal spirit in an instant flown,
Escaped the struggling pangs of death's dread strife.
Repentance, if delay'd to life's last days,
Had it been here delay'd had never come.
Take warning ye survivors, your delays
May cut you off from gaining heaven, your home.

The burial grounds date at least to the 1740s, as shown by the grave-markers of Naphthali Byram and Phoebe Byram, who died in 1747 and 1748. Many markers date from the Revolutionary War period, since Mendham was located close to the Continental Army stationed at Jockey Hollow in Morristown. During an epidemic of smallpox, the church was even used as a hospital. In memory to the twenty-seven soldiers who died from smallpox in 1777 and were buried in unmarked graves, the citizens of Mendham in 1927 placed a stone with the following epitaph to mark their graves:

In Memorian
A.D. 1777
In the Old Church
on present site
A Camp Hospital
for the American Army
27 soldiers
Who Died of Smallpox
Lie Buried Here
Erected 1927

An interesting story is told about the part of the burial ground that has a stone wall around it. In the 1700s, many of Mendham's residents

owned taverns and produced applejack, or "Jersey Lightning." The local
ministers constantly denounced the citizenry for encouraging drinking by
owning so many distilleries and taverns. When it came time for a local
tavern keeper, William Phoenix, to apply for a burial plot at Hilltop Cemetery, his request was turned down by the church fathers. He retaliated by
purchasing an adjoining piece of land near the church burial yard, and
erected a stone wall around it. Over the years the attitude toward tavern
keepers has changed, and William Phoenix's plot became part of the current burial ground.

Planning your visit: The grounds are open to visitors during daylight
hours. For further information, call the church at (201) 543-4012.

18 ❧ *Whippany Burial Ground*
Whippany
1718

Directions: From Interstate 287 north, exit at Route 10 and proceed east toward
New York. The burial ground will be on your right, just past the Troy Hills Road
exit. Turn into the driveway just past the grounds and walk across a wooden bridge
to reach the site. It is open to the public and maintained by the town of Hanover.

Today Whippany Burial Ground is located along fast-moving Route 10,
but back in the 1700s it was situated along a simple country road. The
burial ground has magnificent old trees scattered throughout, and the
Whippany River flows along the far end of it. Years ago, a meetinghouse
was also at this site, but it has long since vanished. The Samuel Tuttle
House, built in 1796, was inadvertently built on a portion of the burial
ground, a mistake not discovered for years; the house is now privately
owned and not open to the public. Tuttle and other family members are
buried in the grounds.

In September 1718, schoolmaster John Richards of Whippany donated the three-and-a-half-acre tract of land to the settlement for a meetinghouse and burial ground. Ironically, three months later he became the
first person to be buried there.

Whippany Burial Ground contains many of the brown sandstone
markers that were carved prior to 1800; most are artistically designed with

37. A closeup of the wonderful angel effigy on the tombstone of Samuel Tuttle (d. 1762, age thirty-eight). Whippany Burial Ground, Whippany.

nice epitaphs. There are more varieties of grim death's heads and cherub-shaped and angel effigies than found in similarly dated burial grounds in northern New Jersey.

The tombstone of an ancestor of former First Lady Barbara Bush can be found around the middle of the grounds. It is a brown sandstone marker of a somber angel effigy with wings, haloed hair, and sad eyes, and is inscribed as follows:

> Here lies the body of Abigail Kitchel
> Deceased Aug 1, 1768
> in the 18 Year of her age
> A blooming youth her Mothers hope
> Like a tender flower grim Death does crown
> Let friends and youth Know they must die
> And meet her in Eternity

The day of my visit, a pretty bow was wrapped around the headstone. The stone, which had been found broken in two, was recently restored at the Metropolitan Museum of Art and now lies among headstones of other Kitchel family members.

Thirteen soldiers and patriots from the Revolutionary War are buried in the Whippany cemetery. One such marker of a private reads:

In Memory of David Cory, who
died July 14, 1811
aged 64 years
My flesh shall slumber in the ground
Till the last trumpet's joyful sound
Then burst the chain with sweet surprise
And in my Savior's Image rise
PVT Continental Line
Revolutionary War
1747–1811

A plaque and a flag mark David Cory's gravesite.

A tombstone marking the burial of a sergeant's wife from the Revolutionary War period is inscribed with the following wonderful epitaph:

In Memory of Phebe Brookfield
wife of Matthias Burnet
who departed this life
Dec 10th 1828
in the 79th year of her age
Almost four score I've lived on Earth
Alas! how short back to my birth
Children and friends prepare for death
You must ere long resign your breath
I've loved and sought your earthly good
And led you to the home of God
Live prudent, virtuous pious lives
And join your friends above the skies

While walking through the grounds, note the gravestone of Colonel Joseph Tuttle, who fought in the French and Indian War and was a county militia commander and church deacon. His five wives are buried nearby as well.

Both the gravemarkers and the epitaphs at Whippany are in well-preserved condition. The community has put much effort into maintaining and restoring this burial ground, especially the New Jersey Historical Society, Daughters of the American Revolution, and the Eagle Scouts.

Planning your visit: The grounds are open to the public during daylight hours.

Other Notable Burial Grounds in Morris County

19 🌤 *Presbyterian Churchyard,* Old Burying Ground, Park Place,
   Morristown.

This cemetery dates from pre–Revolutionary War times, and prominent
families of early local settlers and soldiers are buried here. There are
several thousand markers, including many older red and brown sandstone markers with interesting epitaphs. The site is filled with history, as
Washington spent much time here during the Revolutionary War while his
men were encamped at Jockey Hollow. About 150 Revolutionary War soldiers are buried here; one of them is General John Doughty, third commander of the U.S. Army. A gate surrounds the area; visits can be arranged
by calling (201) 538-1776.

20 🌤 *Dover Quaker Meetinghouse Burial Ground,* Quaker Church
   Road and Quaker Road, off Route 10, Randolph.

Open for visitors at noon every Sunday, or call (201) 361-9427 for an appointment. The area is called Mount Pleasant Hill; the meetinghouse and
burial grounds are on a hill with a nice view of the valleys below. The
square meetinghouse was built in 1758 and contained separate areas for
men, women, and slaves. The white markers are a simple style, in accordance with Quaker tradition.

Passaic County

21 🌤 *Ringwood Manor and Burial Ground*
   Ringwood
   1700s

Directions: From Garden State Parkway, take Exit 153 to Route 46 west. Exit at
Route 23 north and continue toward Pompton. Follow signs for Wanaque and Ringwood, which will lead to Route 511. Stay on 511 all the way to the signs for Ringwood Manor State Park, near the New York state border.

Now a national historic landmark located within Ringwood State Park, the
entire area around the manor has a fascinating past. George Washington

38. View of the Ringwood Manor House, as seen from the burial grounds.

often stopped here, and iron mines dating back to the 1700s once dotted the area. The manor house, built in 1807, has a Victorian-style garden and a lead fountain from Versailles in the back. The burial ground is not noticeable from the manor house but can be found by walking to the back of the house, through the gardens, and up some steps that lead to a dirt road.

The quiet walk to the grounds will take you past large hemlock, sycamore, and elm trees. Shortly after going over a wooden bridge, you will see an assortment of tombstones on your left and down an incline. Robert Erskine's brick crypt is farther down the road; next to it is the crypt of his secretary, Robert Monteith. During the American Revolution, Erskine was brought over from Scotland for his mathematical, engineering, and drafting skills, which were sorely needed to manage the mines. The mines became doubly important when large amounts of iron ore were needed to make iron stoves, tools, and weapons for the war. George Washington used Ringwood as a stopover between West Point and Morristown, and, needing a surveyor, appointed Erskine the official geographer to the army. During his tenure, Robert Erskine drew over one hundred military maps that were used to show troop movements. He died of complications due to exposure while on a map-surveying trip in 1780. Washington planted an elm tree near his grave as a tribute to his friend; unfortunately a twentieth-century storm destroyed the tree.

At one time, the ghost of Erskine was said to be regularly seen on top of his tomb, but the visits apparently stopped when the tombstone was repaired. (See "Ghost Stories and Legends," Part I.) There are said to be five hundred graves between the pond and the road, but only an assortment of fieldstones, and perhaps thirty larger gravemarkers of sandstone and marble, remain. Some inscriptions are not legible, but others have

39. The replacement top to Robert Erskine's brick vault. Years ago, his ghost was said to have haunted the area, sitting on top of the tombstone, holding a blue lantern.

been restored. A few markers lie on the ground, broken off from their bases. Names appearing on the stones are Patterson, Babcock, Bird, and Essex—families that settled in the area in the 1700s and 1800s. Among the five hundred graves are the unmarked remains of Indians, slaves, and ironworkers.

The following inscription is on the sandstone marker of an Irishman most likely brought over to work in the mines:

> Here lies the body of Mical Rynolds
> Born in Ireland near Mullengar
> Dec July 16, 1763 aged 30 years

If you walk down the hill toward the pond, you will find the three marble box tombs of the original Hewitts—John, his wife Ann, and their son John, all of whom died between 1867 and 1870. The tomb of John Hewitt, Jr., describes that he was "trustee of the Public School of the 5th Ward in the City of New York." The three marble tombs are off the dirt road, next to what is locally referred to as "Sallie's Pond," which is kept stocked for fishing. The day I was there, a man and young boy were placidly fishing in the pond, just yards away from the burial ground. It was not hard to imagine that this pastoral setting has been the source of ghost stories.

Succeeding owners of the manor house included Peter Cooper (founder of Cooper Union) and Abram Hewitt. The Hewitts eventually increased the size of the house to fifty-one rooms. The last of the Hewitts to live there were Abram Hewitt's three children: Sarah (called Sallie), Eleanor, and Erskine Hewitt. In 1936 Erskine Hewitt and Norvin Hewitt Green donated Ringwood Manor, the grounds, and its exquisite furnishings to the state of New Jersey. Its beauty and grandeur exist as a lasting tribute to the ironmaster era of the state.

Planning your visit: Ringwood Manor is part of the New Jersey State Park system, so there is a five-dollar entrance fee per car, beginning during the summer season. This charge is discontinued after Labor Day. Besides seeing the burial grounds and manor, plan to spend the day hiking, picnicking, or fishing. The manor house is closed from November until Memorial Day, but it is worth a visit: it has interesting wood-paneled rooms, a Delft-tiled fireplace, and Hudson River–style paintings. It is furnished in styles that span the years 1810 to 1930. Part of the manor contains an art gallery, so call ahead for special events that may be planned during the year. The manor house has limited tours from November until Memorial Day; call ahead for days and times. For more information, call (201) 962-7031.

Other Notable Burial Grounds in Passaic County

22 ⁌ Wanaque Burial Ground, Ringwood Avenue, Wanaque.
This old plot from the 1700s contains about twenty markers. The markers are made from sandstone and marble and contain some interesting inscriptions. Of the families represented here are the Van Wagoners. The cemetery plot is in the woods near St. Francis of Assisi Church.

23 ⁌ Preakness Reformed Dutch Cemetery, Church Lane, Wayne.
On site are hundreds of tombstones dating from the early 1800s. Many old sandstone markers with nice epitaphs of early Dutch families such as Terhune, Hopper, Van Riper, and Dey.

Sussex County

24 ⁌ *Bevans/Peters Valley Cemetery*
    Bevans
    1838

Directions: Go Route 206 north through Stokes State Forest and turn onto Route 521 toward Layton to Peters Valley or Bevans. Go through the town and look for a sign on the side of the road marking the Reformed Church of Bevans. The cemetery sits up on a hill and has a two-story church next to it.

This picturesque community is right in the middle of the Delaware Water Gap Recreation Area, and nearby Peters Valley Artists Center. The Flatbrook-Roy Wildlife Management Area is also in Bevans and attracts many species of songbirds and waterfowl. The cemetery in Bevans is a good site for birdwatchers as well as graveyard enthusiasts. As is the case

with many old cemeteries, it sits high on a hill, and a winding dirt road
leads up to it. Though not as old as some of the other burial grounds in
Sussex County, Bevans has some unusually ornate gravemarkers with detailed designs. Several hundred tombstone markers dating from the 1800s
surround the church. A few markers have small flags next to them, indicating that a soldier is buried there. The inscribed symbols on the marble
tombstones reflect the Victorian era—flowers, leaves, vines, and wreaths.

My favorite gravemarker is one of a large tree, made from hollowed
white bronze and standing about ten feet tall. This type of gravemarker
symbolizes the tree of life and can be found throughout the state. This
particular marker, however, is unusually large, and was made for members of the Rosenkrans family.

The Anna Marvin gravemarker, near the church, is a rectangular mar-

40. A large late nineteenth-
century monument in the
shape of a tree trunk, for
the Rosenkrans family
members. Bevans/Peters
Valley Cemetery, Bevans.

ble marker with intricately carved delicate flowers in both corners at the top. Underneath the flowers is a curved border around an open book. Under the open book are the boldly carved letters, "ANNA":

Wife of Henry Marvin
died January 14th, 1851
Aged 69 years
5 months 2 days

The gravemarkers are not signed, but there is a similar style to many of them, meaning that they were probably carved by the same unknown stonecarver. Other names appearing on tombstones include Berk, Stoll, Bevans, and Snook.

Planning your visit: The churchyard is open to the public during daylight hours. For further information, call (908) 948-5818. While in Bevans, be sure to visit the nearby Peters Valley Craft Center, home of artists who live and work in the community and display their works at the center, as well as the Flatbrook-Roy Wildlife Area.

Other Notable Burial Grounds in Sussex County

25 ❧ *Old Dutch Reformed Cemetery,* Old Mine Road and Flatbrookville Road near the Delaware River, Flatbrookville.
There is much history in this area, which was once surveyed by Robert Erskine, surveyor-general under George Washington. The location is peaceful and deserted in what was once a well-populated area in the 1700s. Old fieldstones and a few tombstones mark the graves of early Dutch and Huguenot settlers. The earliest is dated 1752.

26 ❧ *Lafayette Cemetery,* Route 15, Lafayette.
The Victorian-style wrought-iron gate and fence are very attractive. The cemetery sits on a hill and is overrun with nearly a hundred groundhog holes. The earliest grave is dated 1793; most others are in the 1800s. The village is making attempts to restore the grounds.

27 ❧ *Minisink Burial Ground,* Old Mine Road, off Route 206, Montague.
Take Old Mine Road for three miles, then look for a lane off to the right

with a bar (two red stripes) across it. Walk 170 steps down the path to the burial ground.

Burials here are of early colonists and Indians and date from 1736 to 1907. Minisink was originally known as the DeSchmidt burial ground, incorporated in 1731. There are about fifty gravemarkers here now, but many others have been vandalized or have disappeared over the years. A sign on the tree reads: "Please respect our ancestors' graves." Minisink has some common fieldstone markers with interesting inscriptions. The only burial after 1907 is for "Pepper, My Dog—1954–1960." Call (201) 383-0027 for further information.

28 ❧ *Old Newton Burial Ground,* Main Street, Newton.
The cemetery covers a large area with thousands of markers dating back to Revolutionary War times. The burial ground was neglected for many years and has only recently been cleaned up.

29 ❧ *Sparta Cemetery,* Route 181, Sparta.
This is an interesting old cemetery dating from Revolutionary War times and containing many sandstone markers and touching epitaphs. Note the epitaph of Michael Dickson, "Husband of Sarah," who died in 1805: it was unusual to identify a man as a husband at that time.

30 ❧ *Walpack Burial Ground,* in Stokes State Forest along the Old
          Mine Road near Tillman's Ravine, Walpack Center.
Here are several hundred tombstones of early settlers dating back to the 1800s. Note the iron markers with ornate designs. The setting of this cemetery, near the Delaware River and Tillman's Ravine, is quite beautiful.

Warren County

31 ❧ *Moravian Burial Ground*
          Hope
          1769

Directions: From Route 80 west toward Pennsylvania, take Exit 12, or Route 521 south, about one mile to the town of Hope. Turn right at the yellow caution light

in the center of town. The Methodist Church will be on your left. The Moravian
Burial Ground is a section to the left in back of the Methodist grounds.

The most startling feature of this early burial ground is that some tombstones lie flat on the ground. At first glance, one might mistake them for
footstones in a path running through the cemetery, but they were pur-
posely set this way by the Moravians in the late 1700s and early 1800s.
Because the markers are only two feet long, it must have seemed sensible
to lay them flat. Over the years they have settled well into the ground, and
now grass clippings and dirt cover parts of most of the forty-odd markers.

The well-ordered life the Moravians led is reflected in the manner in
which the gravestones were recorded. Every one of the stones is numbered and follows a chronological list of burials, beginning with number
1 in 1768. Multiple burials are represented by some of the stones, while
others indicate only one burial. The numbers were originally at the top of
each stone, but many of them have become obliterated or worn. All of the
stones in this burial ground have been copied and are listed in the Moravian Archives in Bethlehem, Pennsylvania. Some simply need to have clippings brushed away to be clearly read:

41. The Moravian Burial
Ground in Hope.
Short, flat marker for
David Tombler (d. 1815),
a member of the Moravian
community that settled in
Hope in the late 1700s. The
Moravians numbered all
their stones; this one is
number 45 (at top).

45
David Tombler
Born Jan 19th, 1771
at New York
departed this life
May 21st 1815

33
Conrad Omensetter
Born Dec 18
1740
In Germany
Departed
July 2, 1792

The Moravians were settlers of mostly German descent who emigrated from Bethlehem to this part of New Jersey in 1769. They called their 1,500-acre settlement "Greenland," and drew up a plan for a communal-type village. They established a tannery, two mills, a tavern, and other joint ventures to become a totally self-sufficient society. Their substantial stone buildings, built from blue limestone, can still be seen near the burial grounds. Some of the deaths here occurred in 1808, the year of a terrible smallpox epidemic. Because of the many fatalities and resulting financial problems, the remaining Moravians left the village of Hope and returned to Bethlehem.

Planning your visit: The village of Hope offers a walking tour. Go to the museum on High Street to find sites to visit. Spend some time in the Methodist section of the grounds, as there are some interesting inscriptions on the tombstones, though most are difficult to read. Both the Methodist and the Moravian grounds are open to the public during daylight hours. For more information, call the Moravian Church at (908) 459-4435.

Other Notable Burial Grounds in Warren County

32 ❧ *Yellow Frame Presbyterian Church Cemetery,* Route 94,
    Yellow Frame.
Across Dark Moon Road is a burial ground dating from the 1700s containing many interesting sandstone markers and epitaphs. They mark the

graves of Revolutionary War soldiers and settlers from the area. The infamous Dark Moon Inn was nearby, where a burial plot was once maintained for gamblers and criminals from the area. No trace remains of these burials, or of the inn.

33 ✺ *Hackettstown Presbyterian Cemetery,* Main Street, Hackettstown. This burial ground and church date back to the late 1700s and contain several hundred tombstones. Many markers are made from sandstone and have interesting designs and epitaphs. A nice tribute to a mourned wife is given on the Patrick family tombstone. Many Revolutionary War soldiers are buried here.

34 ✺ *Old Christian Church Cemetery,* Allamuchy Road, Johnsonburg. Burials date from the late 1700s. The cemetery is well known for the marker and remains of Joseph Thomas, called "The White Pilgrim" minister. Because of a controversy that existed at the time of his death in 1835, his family was not allowed to bury him in these grounds. But eleven years later, the church members changed their minds and his remains were moved here. His tall monument stands in the back of the grounds. (See "Ghost Stories and Legends.")

35 ✺ *Calno Burial Ground,* Old Mine Road, Pahaquarry.
This is an abandoned cemetery with about 150 burials, but many fewer tombstones due to vandalism. Many early Dutch family names can be found here: Van Campen, Ribble, and DePew, among others. It is located near the Van Campen Inn and by old copper mines along the Delaware River. The grounds are in the process of being restored by a descendant of the Van Campen family.

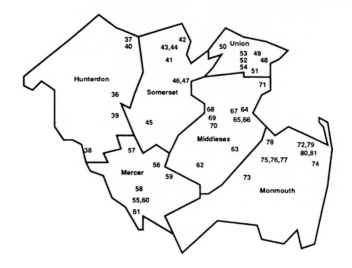

Central New Jersey

Hunterdon County

36 Flemington—Case Burial Ground
37 Fairmount—Fairmount Presbyterian Church Burial Ground
38 Lambertville—First Presbyterian Church Cemetery
39 Larisons Corners—Rockefeller Family Burial Ground
40 Oldwick—Zion Lutheran Church Cemetery

Somerset County

41 Pluckemin—Pluckemin Presbyterian Church Burial Ground
42 Basking Ridge—Presbyterian Church Cemetery
43 Bedminster—Old Bedminster Churchyard
44 Bedminster—Cowperthwaite African-American Burial Ground
45 Neshanic—Neshanic Cemetery Association
46 Somerville—Old Dutch Parsonage Burial Ground
47 Somerville—Somerville Burial Ground

Union County

48 Elizabeth—First Presbyterian Church Burial Ground
49 Union—Connecticut Farms Presbyterian Church Burial Ground
50 New Providence—Presbyterian Church Cemetery
51 Rahway—First Presbyterian Cemetery
52 Scotch Plains—Baptist Church Burial Ground
53 Springfield—First Presbyterian Church Cemetery
54 Westfield—Presbyterian Church Burial Ground

Mercer County

55 Trenton—St. Michael's Church Burial Ground
56 Princeton—Princeton Cemetery

57 Hopewell—Old School Baptist Church Cemetery
58 Lawrenceville—Presbyterian Church Cemetery
59 Princeton—Princeton Baptist Church Cemetery
60 Trenton—First Presbyterian Church Cemetery
61 Trenton—Riverview Cemetery

Middlesex County

62 Cranbury—First Presbyterian Burial Ground
63 Spotswood—St. Peter's Episcopal Church Cemetery
64 Woodbridge—First Presbyterian Church Burial Ground
65 Edison—St. James Episcopal Churchyard
66 Edison—Stelton Baptist Churchyard
67 Metuchen—First Presbyterian Church Cemetery
68 New Brunswick—Christ Episcopal Churchyard
69 New Brunswick—First Reformed Church Cemetery
70 North Brunswick—Van Liew Cemetery
71 Perth Amboy—St. Peter's Episcopal Church Burial Ground

Monmouth County

72 Middletown—Presbyterian Burial Ground
73 Tennent—Old Tennent Church Cemetery
74 Shrewsbury—Christ Church Burial Ground
75 Marlboro—Old Brick Reformed Church Cemetery
76 Marlboro—Old Scots Burial Ground
77 Marlboro—Old Topanemus Burying Ground
78 Matawan—Mount Pleasant Cemetery
79 Middletown—Baptist Church Burial Ground
80 Middletown—Christ Episcopal Church Burial Ground
81 Middletown—Reformed Church Burial Ground

Central New Jersey

Hunterdon County

36 🍂 *Case Burial Ground*
Flemington
1774

Directions: From Route 31 or 202 follow signs to Flemington and go to Main Street. From Main Street turn onto Mine Street, make a right to Park Street and a left to Bonnell. The burial ground is about two blocks farther on Bonnell Street.

The most startling fact about the Case Burial Ground is its location. Less than a hundred feet wide, this burial ground is in the middle of a residential area. In the 1700s, this area contained only woods and a handful of settlers. John Philip Case was the town's first settler, and the current site on Bonnell Street was his family's burial ground. Today the grounds consist of several dozen tombstones positioned between two houses. If the burial ground were not there, no doubt a home would be in its place.

The tombstones are dated from 1774 to 1856, and some of their inscriptions are illegible. One of the more legible ones is of mottled limestone and says:

In Memory of Peter Case
who died
Sept. 25th 1796
Aged 45 years
Removed Aug 3 1856

The marker indicates it was moved to its present location from somewhere else, or it may have been left as a cenotaph, with the body removed for unknown reasons in 1856.

Another granite tombstone is of the common headboard shape, and shows some signs of damage at the corners. The inscription reads:

> In Memory of SUSANNAH
> The Wife of John Schenck
> Who departed this Life
> October 20, 1782
> Aged 20 years

The most interesting marker at Case was erected for a Delaware Indian named Tuccamirgan who helped the first white settler, John Case, adapt to the unfamiliar land and life-style in the 1700s. Case would not have survived without this Indian's help, and the two men became close friends. After Case died, his Indian friend requested to be buried next to him. His request was honored, and in typical Indian custom, Tuccamirgan was buried in an upright, sitting position. The Indian's original marker disappeared over the years; in 1925 the citizens of Flemington replaced it with a large marble monument, which says: "In Memory of The Delaware Indian Chief Tuccamirgan 1750."

Planning your visit: Be sure to visit the surrounding area, as it has many historic buildings. Near the burial ground on 5 Bonnell Street is the Fleming Castle built in 1756. This is not actually a castle, but an interesting home and inn built by Samuel Fleming, for whom the town was named. The building is now owned by the Daughters of the American Revolution.

Other Notable Burial Grounds in Hunterdon County

37 ❧ Fairmount Presbyterian Church Burial Ground, Fairmount.
This burial ground contains several hundred marble, iron, sandstone, and bronze tombstones, some having wonderful epitaphs. Gray marble stones dating from the 1760s and 1770s are for the Waldorf and Kreter family members. Seven Civil War and Revolutionary War tombstones are located here.

42. A replacement marker for the Delaware chief, Tuccamirgan, who helped John Case, the area's first white settler, survive the winter. The chief was buried in an upright sitting position in Case Burial Ground in 1750.

38 ❧ *First Presbyterian Church Cemetery*, North Union Street,
    Lambertville.

Behind this church, which dates from the early 1800s, lies a small, forgotten cemetery. In those days Lambertville was known as Coryell's Ferry and was one of the few points where one could cross the Delaware River. Here is the gravestone of George Coryell, the last survivor of the six men who had lain George Washington in his tomb. Other markers date from the late 1700s to early 1800s.

39 ❧ *Rockefeller Family Burial Ground*, Route 202, Larisons Corners.

These grounds are part of the United Presbyterian Cemetery. Many markers are for descendants of German-born Johann Peter Rockefeller, though he himself is thought to be buried on a nearby farm. A ten-foot granite monument was erected for him in 1906 by a descendant.

40 ❧ *Zion Lutheran Church Cemetery*, High Street, Oldwick.

The cemetery is in the center of town, part of a beautiful community surrounded by rolling hills. Oldwick contains the oldest continuous Lutheran

43. The monument for Johann Peter Rockefeller (d. 1763) was erected in 1906 in the Rockefeller Family Burial Ground, United Presbyterian Cemetery, Larisons Corners. This example of an early postcard is postmarked 1909.
(Author's collection.)

congregation in northern New Jersey, dating from 1749. The tombstones date from the mid-1700s; some are even inscribed in German. Read the epitaph for Baltes Pickel, who died in 1766, warning men "not to dig too near."

Somerset County

41 ❧ *Pluckemin Presbyterian Church Burial Ground*
Pluckemin
1757

Directions: From Interstate 287 north in New Brunswick, take Route 78 east to Routes 202/206. Follow signs to Pluckemin. The highway will bring you right to the church in the center of town.

The quaint village of Pluckemin has been in a long-standing dispute over the origin of the word "pluckemin." Some authorities believe it stems from the Indian word meaning "persimmon," while others insist it was due to an innkeeper who would stand in the middle of town to solicit customers, or to "pluck-em-in." Either way, Pluckemin retains its small-town atmosphere. Around the Presbyterian Church on Main Street stand many older homes with large porches.

Several hundred gravemarkers dot the churchyard. The oldest markers, of red and brown sandstone, light coarse-grained granite, and grayish-white marble, are to the right of the front of the church. Some markers have corresponding footstones with initials or dates inscribed on them. Several gravemarkers in this same area are made of crude fieldstone and have no inscriptions. A very attractive sandstone tombstone for Robert Eoff, who died in 1814, stands here. It has a fan-shaped motif carved on top, small rosettes on the sides, and delicately carved leaf fronds at the bottom. The stonecarver is unknown. The lovely epitaph proclaims:

> In Memory of Robert Eoff who departed this life
> April the 20th 1814 in the 75th year of his age
> Like as a shadow or the morning dew
> My days are spent which were but few
> Grieve not for me dear wife it is in vain
> Your loss I hope is my eternal gain

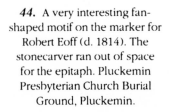

44. A very interesting fan-shaped motif on the marker for Robert Eoff (d. 1814). The stonecarver ran out of space for the epitaph. Pluckemin Presbyterian Church Burial Ground, Pluckemin.

Other markers tell us about Revolutionary War soldiers who are buried here. Most are Americans, but a few are British. Back then the church was known as St. Paul's Lutheran Church and was used as a temporary prison for about 230 British soldiers. These men were detained at St. Paul's after the Battle of Princeton. One of the most notable and handsome marble tombstones reads:

In Memory of the Honble
Captn Willm Leslie of 17th British Regiment, son of the
Earl of Leven in Scotland
He fell Jan 3 1777 aged 26 yrs at
Battle of Princeton
His friend Benjn Rush of Philadelphia haht caused
this Stone to be erected as a mark of his esteem for
his worth and of his respect for his noble family.

45. Even though Captain Leslie fought and died for the British at the Battle of Princeton in 1777, his grave in Pluckemin Presbyterian Church Burial Ground has been marked with a United States veteran's emblem and flag.

(Benjamin Rush was an eminent physician during the Revolutionary War.)
    Another epitaph on the marker of the Teeple headstone tells the story of an elderly couple who died on the same day:

Teeple John born Oct 29, 1728 died March 17, 1813
within 3 hours of wife Margaret born July 15, 1737,
died March 17, 1813.

One of the earlier tombstones in the churchyard belongs to an elderly German couple, John and Catherine Melick, who died within a month of each other in 1763. The stone shown in figure 6 is in the Melick family plot. Jacob and Mary Magdalene Eoff are buried here as well, Mary having died in 1761. The Eoffs ran a popular inn across the street from the church called Eoff's Tavern. In 1777 George Washington stopped here to write to Congress about his victory in the Battle of Princeton. The entire area was the hub of social activity during Revolutionary War days. Though Pluckemin still retains its small-town atmosphere, patriots from those early days would hardly recognize the old town, which now lies within a mile from two of New Jersey's major highways, Interstates 78 and 287.

Planning your visit: The burial grounds are unfenced and open to the public. Park in the church parking lot off Route 202. Walk from the parking lot around to the far right of the church to view the older tombstones. For further information, contact the church at (908) 658-3346.

Other Notable Burial Grounds in Somerset County

42 ❧ *Presbyterian Church Cemetery,* West Oak Street, Basking Ridge. Graves of early Scotch Presbyterian settlers with tombstones dating from 1717. This is the former site of the famous Basking Ridge Oak, where George Washington stopped to rest back in the late 1700s, when the tree was already said to be a hundred years old.

43 ❧ *Old Bedminster Churchyard,* Routes 202/206, just north of Interstate 287, Bedminster.
This was the former site of the Dutch Reformed Church. Here are hundreds of graves from the 1700s and 1800s with red sandstone markers and interesting epitaphs. Of historical interest is that years ago, the church rejected two people for burial in the yard: one was a woman who was denied burial because she was insane, and the other was an infant who was denied burial because her father was a Congregationalist. These two were buried outside the churchyard's boundaries, but years later, the church accepted the outcasts for inclusion into the churchyard itself.

44 🙞 *Cowperthwaite African-American Burial Ground,* Route 523
   or Lamington Road, near the intersection of Cowperthwaite Road,
   Lamington.

These settlers were said to be descendants of slaves in the area. Independent and free in the 1800s, they purchased the land for burial purposes. There are about fifteen gravemarkers, with names including Bray, Layton, and Pierson. Some markers represent multiple burials. Note the crude fieldstone markers with no inscriptions. An African-American Civil War soldier, William Van Horn, U.S. Colored Troops, who died in 1887, is buried here.

46. One of the many crude
fieldstones in Neshanic
Cemetery. This one is for
Elisabeth DeMot (d. 1763).
Note the backward *s.*

45 ∾ *Neshanic Cemetery Association,* Amwell Road, Route 514, east
  of Neshanic.

Here is a picturesque site on a hill overlooking the south branch of the
Raritan River with graves dating from the 1700s. Here one can find wonderful examples of early fieldstones with crude inscriptions, the oldest dating back to 1763. This is also a good bird-watching area.

46 ∾ *Old Dutch Parsonage Burial Ground,* Washington Place,
  Somerville.

Built in 1751, the parsonage is now a historical museum. In the back of the
museum are graves from the 1700s, including those of Revolutionary War
soldiers. Be sure to visit the parsonage for its historic exhibits.

47 ∾ *Somerville Burial Ground,* South Bridge Street, Route 206,
  Somerville.

On both sides of the road are old burial grounds of early Dutch settlers in
the area. The oldest stones border the front, quite close to the stone wall.
Many of the sandstone markers bear familiar names of early Dutch settlers
and soldiers such as Hardenburgh, Voorhees, and Freylingheysen. Many
of their descendants still reside in the area.

Union County

48 ∾ *First Presbyterian Church Burial Ground*
  Elizabeth
  1761

Directions: From the New Jersey Turnpike, take Exit 13 and follow Route 439
(Bayway Avenue) to Broad Street. Take a right onto Broad Street. Follow Broad
Street to the downtown area. The church is on the left just past the courthouse.
Metered parking is available right next to the grounds on Caldwell Place.

The attractive Georgian-style church and burial ground are amid modern
stores, parking lots, and office buildings, and next to the Union County
Courthouse. Dating back to a period when the city was known as Elizabethtown, the church and surrounding area were along the well-traveled
King's Highway. Elizabeth was an important link between New York and

Trenton, and even served as the state's first colonial capital from about 1665 to 1686. During Revolutionary War times, the Reverend James Caldwell would preach to his congregation with loaded pistols and sentries outside, in case the British attacked during his sermon. He became known as "the fighting parson." Both James and Hannah Caldwell, his wife, were shot by British soldiers and buried in this Presbyterian cemetery. A monument now stands in their memory. (See also Connecticut Farms Presbyterian Church Burial Ground, Union, for more of their story.)

Glancing around today, it is hard to imagine what the area must have looked like in the 1600s and 1700s. The cemetery is quite picturesque, but a small-village atmosphere no longer exists: the church and grounds are now in a highly urbanized area. In the driveway behind the burial ground is a garbage zone. Just feet away from the tombstones are stacks of garbage, waiting to be picked up by contractors. Many of the tombstones lean over and are broken. The burial ground has no fence around it, and a few homeless people were lying near some stones the day I visited. In spite of the few negatives, it remains one of the most interesting cemeteries in the state.

The tombstones at the cemetery show the Puritan concepts popular in Elizabethtown in colonial days. There are over two thousand tombstones, crypts, and monuments erected to honor the citizens of this oldest English-speaking settlement in New Jersey. The gravemarkers are representative of the styles of early New York/New Jersey stonecarvers. Many are signed, and show good examples of the motifs and designs discussed in chapter 3.

Some of the stonecarvers represented here are Jonathan Hand Osborne, Ebenezer Price, David Jeffries, Aaron Ross, Isaac Ross, and Jonathan Akin. The earliest style found is the rare death's head and crossed bones with the hourglass symbol. Most common on the carvings predating 1750 are the death's head and soul effigies. The angel and cherub effigies are most predominant among the tombstones after 1750.

Allow enough time to read the interesting epitaphs on many of these markers, such as the following:

> A fabric once on Earth I was
> And nothing Else but dust
> I'm gone to Join the Heavenly tribe
> And with my God to Rest
> *(tombstone by an unknown carver for Frances Watkins,*
> *who died in 1787 at the age of fifty-seven)*

47. This wonderful gravestone for Charity Price (d. 1776) was probably carved by David Jeffries. The epitaph is topped by a stern-faced soul effigy with crown, and is surrounded by tulips and vines that frame the inscription.

On the double headstone of Hannah Hendricks and her son David, both of whom died in 1732, is inscribed:

> Adieu vain World our dearest Friends farewel
> Prepare with us in this dark House to dwell
> Till ye last Trump our ruin'd Frame repair
> At Christ's Descent to meet him in ye air.

As one reads these epitaphs, it becomes obvious that many colonists died well before their time. The following is an example:

> In the Bloom of her Life
> Adorned with every outward Grace
> Enriched with every Christian virtue
> She, bid adieu to Earth and went to Heaven
> 'Twas the Survivor died
> Grief-worn traveller
> Go, learn Submission to the will of God
> Permanent Felicity is not
> For Man on Earth.

The tombstones in this burial ground show the damaging effects of weathering and pollution, perhaps due to the chemical plants and other industries located in the general area. The signs of weathering are obvious when one examines the landmark book *Gravestone Designs,* by Emily Wasserman, written in 1972. The photos of intact tombstones in this book are proof of a rapid deterioration of the stones within a span of twenty years.

Planning your visit: The present church on the burial ground dates from 1784; the original structure was destroyed by fire. It is the only historic building in the immediate area, but other historic buildings can be found in Elizabeth. The burial ground is open to the public. To visit the church or arrange for a tour, call (201) 353-1518. The train station is within walking distance, and bus transportation is available. For a concise record of many of the headstones as they appeared in 1892, including photos and sketches, consult the book *Inscriptions on Tombstones: Elizabeth, New Jersey,* by William Ogden Wheeler and Edmund D. Halsey.

49 ☙ *Connecticut Farms Presbyterian Church Burial Ground*
Union
1732

Directions: Take the Garden State Parkway to Exit 139B. Follow the exit ramp under the bridge and take a quick left onto Chestnut Street. The church driveway will be on your immediate right. Drive in and go all the way to the back of the lot near the burial ground.

The quaint brick church, built in 1788, replaced the original one burned down by British soldiers during the Revolutionary War. This church was the first building in New Jersey to be placed on the National Register of Historic Places. The adjacent burial ground contains many interesting sandstone markers with wonderful examples of death's head and angel effigies dating from 1732. Most stones are in fine condition, with very readable epitaphs and inscriptions. Some of the carvings were done by J. C. Mooney, Jonathan Osborne, E. P. Price, and J. Tucker, active stonecutters in the area. Many stories are told in these inscriptions, such as:

> In Memory of Aaron & Phebe
> Son & daughter of Joseph &
> Nancy Bonnel. Aaron died
> Aug. 25, 1793 aged 8 years
> 11 months & 10 days. Phebe died
> Dec 10th 1789, aged 1 year 2 mo
> & 10 days.
> I take these little Lambs said He
> And lay them in my breast
> Protection they shall find in me
> In me be ever blest.

This epitaph appears on a double marker made of red sandstone used to mark the site of two burials occurring four years apart. The stone was signed by J. C. Mooney. It was not uncommon to place a marker on a grave long after a person died. Settlers commonly lost many children to childhood diseases that are no longer a plague. The chances of a child's reaching adulthood in the late 1700s to early 1800s was only 50 percent.

Connecticut Farms is filled with tombstones containing wonderful designs and motifs of the period: the tulip design, crossed saber swords, hearts, birds, the sun and moon, and angel effigies with crowns, among others.

48. Crossed swords motif
from the gravestone of
Revolutionary War veteran
John Allen (d. 1826,
age sixty-five).
Connecticut Farms
Presbyterian
Burial Ground, Union.
(Courtesy Emily Wasserman,
*Gravestone Designs, Rubbings,
and Photographs from Early New
York and New Jersey,* New York:
Dover Publications, 1972.)

The crossed swords design is on the marker of Captain John Allen, who died in 1826 at age sixty-five. The swords indicate his status as a soldier during the Revolutionary War. His epitaph gives a warning to viewers to not waste time on earth, as death is always waiting for us:

> Let this vain world engage no more
> Behold the gaping tomb:
> It bids you seize the perfect hour
> Tomorrow Death may come.

Smallpox killed thousands of settlers in the colonies, and the technique of inoculation was not safe until Edward Jenner successfully developed a smallpox vaccine in 1796. Before then, inoculations were still attempted, as the following epitaph, carved by E. P. Price, tells us:

> HERE lies the Body
> of David Maxsell
> who died of ye Small
> Pox by Innoculation
> March ye Anno
> Domini 1763 In the
> 37th Year of his Age

The settlers in Union had emigrated from Connecticut. The tombstones contain names such as Osborn, Baldwin, Earl, Brant, Higgins, Headley, Crane, Thompson, Sayre, Bunnel, Clark, Potter, among others. Some were innocent victims of the war, when fighting broke out and the village was burned. The British swept through the area, proceeding to

49. The marker for Ann Wade (d. 1737, age eighty-eight) shows a
broad-faced angel effigy with recessed facial features and a crown.
Connecticut Farms Presbyterian Burial Ground, Union.

Springfield and other towns. Reverend James Caldwell had moved his
family here from Elizabeth during the war to get them away from danger.
Unfortunately, when fighting began in the area, Hannah Caldwell, Reverend Caldwell's wife, was killed by a British soldier as she was sitting in the
parsonage. The parsonage is still across the street, and now houses the
Union County Historical Society. Hannah and her husband were buried in
the First Presbyterian Church Burial Ground in Elizabeth, rather than at
Connecticut Farms.

The inscriptions have been copied and can be found in the Union
County Historical Society and in the Alexander Library Archives at Rutgers
University.

Allow yourself plenty of time to walk through this attractive burial
ground to read the many epitaphs that give vignettes of life in colonial
times.

Planning your visit: This burial ground is surrounded by a wrought-iron
fence and has a gate with a combination lock. Arrange a visit ahead of
time by calling (908) 688-3164.

Other Notable Burial Grounds in Union County

50 **Presbyterian Church Cemetery,** Springfield Avenue, New
Providence.
Directly behind this church are about one thousand gravemarkers dating
back to 1784. The grounds contain nice landscaping, with birch, maple,
and sycamore trees. Many of the markers are made of sandstone, granite,
and marble, and there are some fieldstones. The DAR has placed markers
on many gravesites, including one for a major general from the War of
1812. A number of motifs are represented on the stones: weeping willow,
flowers, falling tree, lamb, urn, wheat. Some gravemarkers were carved by
A. Willcox, a noted carver from central New Jersey. The church has a copy
of the inscriptions with a map by Hugh B. Jordan.

51 **First Presbyterian Cemetery,** St. Georges Avenue, Rahway.
Across from the famed Merchants and Drovers Tavern dating from the
1700s are this church and cemetery. Hundreds of tombstones here date all
the way back to the Revolutionary War period. Some stones were carved
by New Jersey stonecarver John Frazee. Abraham Clark, a signer of the
Declaration of Independence, was buried here in 1794.

52 **Baptist Church Burial Ground,** God's Acre, Grand and Union
Streets, Scotch Plains.
Here are hundreds of tombstones, some dating from the 1700s. Many were
carved by Jonathan Hand Osborne, a well-known stonecutter who lived
in the town. The earliest crude fieldstone dates from 1754 and was erected
for Sarah Frazee. Note the fascinating design on the stone of Benjamin
Lambert, who died in 1761. It shows a tree being cut down with a hatchet,
nearby a mass of clouds. Find the two burials and lengthy epitaphs of
former slaves: "Caesar, an African who died Feb 7, 1806 at age 104," and
David Allen Drake, "Born a Slave . . . Died a Freeman."

53 **First Presbyterian Church Cemetery,** Morris Avenue, Springfield.
The church and grounds were the site of a battle during the Revolutionary
War, and a monument commemorates the event. The Reverend Caldwell
of Elizabeth took part in this battle, just two weeks after his wife was killed
by the British at Connecticut Farms (Union). Some stones here were

carved by J. C. Mooney and David Jeffries. Note the tombstones of the
Poole brothers, who were on opposite sides during the Civil War.

54 ⁊ Presbyterian Church Burial Ground, Mountain Avenue, Westfield.
This burial ground is also called Colonial Cemetery and was a source of
inspiration for the humorist Charles Addams. He grew up in Westfield and
visited the cemetery often. His macabre humor created "The Addams
Family" series, along with cartoons for *The New Yorker* magazine. Here
can be found hundreds of tombstones dating from the late 1700s. There
are many sandstone markers, some by J. Tucker, whose style resembled
Jonathan Osborne's. Soldiers from several wars are buried here.

Mercer County

55 ⁊ St. Michael's Church Burial Ground
Trenton
1753

Directions: From Route 1 south in Trenton, take the Perry Street exit. Turn right
onto Broad Street and left onto North Warren. Proceed on this one-way street to
140 North Warren.

St. Michael's is now an inner-city church and burial ground surrounded by
wrought-iron gates a few blocks away from the historic Battle Monument.
This monument marks the spot where Washington's men opened fire
against the British on December 26, 1776. St. Michael's Church had been
in existence for about thirty years at that time, and the church walls sus-
tained much damage. The interior was also damaged while Hessian troops
were quartered in the church during the war. The building was rebuilt
many times over the years and was eventually covered with tan-colored
stucco. The once larger cemetery was split into three sections, all on different sides of the building. Today about one hundred tombstones exist,
mostly made from white sandstone or marble, with urn-shaped tops. By
the 1920s the gravemarkers and burial grounds were in rough shape and
some restoration work was needed. The congregation raised $1,500 to
have the eighteenth- and nineteenth-century stones cleaned and have the
inscriptions recut to make them readable. Some of the oldest stones are of

50. A lonely marble dove perches on top of the monument for Pauline Joseph Ann Holton (d. 1820). Pauline was the daughter of Joseph Bonaparte, King of Spain, and his Quaker mistress, Annette Savage.

Trenton's earliest citizens, such as the Coxe and Williams families. These can be seen in the locked burial grounds on the right side of the church. Because of church expansion on this side, some of the tombstones are embedded into the outside walls of the church. The actual remains are underneath the newer church additions. To visit the markers on the left side of the church, you must enter through another locked gate on the left. The first noticeable marker is a tall white marble monument, surrounded by a small iron fence and much brush and weeds in the enclosure. A lonely white marble dove sits on top of a carved funerary urn at the top of the monument. On the bottom is inscribed:

Erected
by a bereft Mother
In the Memory
of a beloved Child
Pauline Joseph Ann Holton
Died in 1820

An interesting story is behind this lonely monument: Pauline Joseph Ann Holton was Napoleon Bonaparte's niece. His brother, Joseph Bonaparte, former king of Spain, lived in nearby Bordentown in 1816. He kept a beautiful Quaker mistress, Annette Savage, in a mansion on Lalor Street in Trenton, while his wife, the former queen, lived far away in Spain. Annette was shunned by society in Trenton, and had a rather lonely existence. Her life became even more unbearable after her daughter Pauline died. Shortly after Pauline's burial at St. Michael's, Joseph Bonaparte took Annette and their other daughter, Charlotte, to upstate New York, where he had a house built for his mistress near Watertown. Bonaparte eventually returned home to his wife in Spain, and Annette married a young Frenchman. The relationship of Annette Savage and Joseph Bonaparte later was recognized when Charlotte was presented in court to Napoleon III.

At the back of the burial ground, beyond Pauline's monument, you will see tombstones leaning against the building and no longer buried in the ground. Proceed farther back through a narrow outside hall in the back and you will arrive at a third burial ground. This hidden section is quite overgrown with grass and weeds and contains markers of a former mayor of Trenton and other important early citizens. Surprisingly, the top of the fence running along the back is electrified. It borders an empty, boarded-up warehouse in the back and a run-down building on the side. It is a stretch of the imagination, but try to picture the more pastoral setting of the nineteenth century, when the grounds were nicely landscaped and the surroundings were more pleasant.

Planning your visit: The burial grounds are kept locked for security reasons. Arrange a visit by calling (609) 392-8086 or visiting St. Michael's around noontime, when the daily services are held. The right side of the burial ground can be seen during service times, as the gate will be open. The left side is always locked, and you must ask to view the two sections on that side. Parking is available directly in front of the church or across the street. A word of caution: poison ivy grows throughout the cemetery, particularly on the left side.

56 ❧ *Princeton Cemetery*
Princeton
1757

Directions: From Route 1 south or north, take Alexander Road to the end into Princeton. Make a right onto Mercer Street and another right onto Nassau Street and proceed to Witherspoon Street. Turn left onto Witherspoon; the burial grounds are two blocks down at the corner of Wiggins and Witherspoon.

Enter through the only unlocked gate off Wiggins and be sure to stop and pick up a cemetery map in the mailbox of the superintendent's house. The map will direct you to some of the gravemarkers of the more prominent gravesites. The grounds are owned by Princeton University and the Nassau Presbyterian Church and contain the graves of famous politicians, eleven college presidents, poets, writers, preachers, and even a United States president and vice president.

The original older section of the burial ground, along Witherspoon and Wiggins Streets, was acquired in 1757 by the College of New Jersey (now Princeton University) shortly after the college had moved here from Newark. The cemetery has long been a favorite place of history enthusiasts, as much of Princeton's past is revealed in this serene setting.

The oldest gravemarkers are of Margaret Leonard, first European child born in Princeton, who died in 1760, and Dickinson Shepard, a student at Nassau Hall at the college, who died in 1761. Both of these are located across from the Presidents' Plot. Nearby these two markers is the tombstone of Guy Chew, a Mohawk Indian who converted to Christianity.

One of the most widely visited sites is called the Presidents' Plot. It is a section bordering Wiggins Street that contains eleven of the former presidents of Princeton University. In this plot are Aaron Burr, Sr., second president of Princeton; Jonathan Edwards, Calvinist theologian; John Witherspoon, a signer of the Declaration of Independence and member of the Continental Congress; and other Princeton University presidents. Their marble-top and brick box-tomb markers are inscribed in Latin. Next to the marker of Aaron Burr, Sr., is the monument for his son, Aaron, Jr.

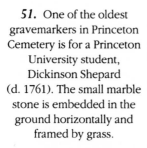

51. One of the oldest gravemarkers in Princeton Cemetery is for a Princeton University student, Dickinson Shepard (d. 1761). The small marble stone is embedded in the ground horizontally and framed by grass.

(see fig. 5), a former vice president of the United States but most often remembered for the famous duel with Alexander Hamilton. In Weehawken, N.J., on the morning of July 11, 1804, Alexander Hamilton was mortally wounded by Aaron Burr. The men had been political enemies for fifteen years.

Princeton Cemetery is also known for its monument to former president Grover Cleveland, who lived in Princeton from 1897 to 1908. Every year on March 13, his birthday, a wreath is sent here from the White House, and a ceremony is held complete with honor guard and firing squad from nearby Fort Dix.

John O'Hara, the famous writer, is also buried at Princeton. His monument reads: "Better than anyone else he told the truth about his time. He wrote honestly and well."

Other scholars buried here are Paul Tulane, for whom Tulane University is named, and John von Neumann, a mathematician and pioneer in the field of computers and cybernetics.

Many interesting epitaphs can be found in Princeton Cemetery. One marker is a memorial for the wife and children of John L. Thompson of Lancaster, Pennsylvania. The marker reads: "They perished in the Hudson River in their attempt to escape the burning of the steamboat Henry Clay on the 28th day of July AD 1852."

One of my all-time favorite epitaphs at Princeton Cemetery is the one for a gentleman which says: "I told you I was sick."

These are only a few of the gravesites in this seventeen-acre cemetery, still in use today. Barbara Sigmund, beloved former mayor of Princeton, who lost her battle with cancer, was one of the most recent to be buried there, in 1990.

Allow plenty of time to visit these spacious grounds filled with historic monuments from the past.

Planning your visit: A map, supplied by the cemetery, is the best way to find the notable gravemarkers here. Look at the map outside the superintendent's house on the cemetery grounds. The superintendent is knowledgeable and helpful, so be sure to ask him any questions about the burial grounds. He is accustomed to the many visitors, many of whom wander in from the nearby shops on Nassau Street. To arrange a tour, call (609) 924-1369.

Other Notable Burial Grounds in Mercer County

57 ☙ Old School Baptist Church Cemetery, West Broad Street, Hopewell. This burial ground dates from 1748, with mostly red sandstone markers. John Hart, a signer of the Declaration of Independence, is buried here. A "Speaking Block," made of granite and sandstone, is there, a reminder of the time when Joab Houghton stood on the block to convince patriots to enlist in the war after the Battle of Lexington.

58 ☙ Presbyterian Church Cemetery, Main Street, Lawrenceville. This burial ground lies next to what was formerly known as the King's Highway. In this wonderful historic area are buildings from the 1700s, including the red brick church built in 1716. The burial ground contains white limestone and marble markers with epitaphs dating from 1764. Also here are markers on gravesites of Revolutionary War soldiers placed by the Daughters of the American Revolution.

59 ❧ Princeton Baptist Church Cemetery, Route 1 and Washington
    Road, Princeton.

Directly behind this church, built in 1814, are about one hundred gravestones, mostly made of white limestone and marble. There is only one
sandstone marker. Note the fancy lettering style on the stone of Joseph
Grover. An Asian congregation now shares the Baptist Church site, a sign
of the emerging population change in the area.

60 ❧ First Presbyterian Church Cemetery, 114 East State Street, Trenton.
Now in the Commons Area of Trenton, this white stucco-on-brick building
contains tombstones of early Trenton citizens and soldiers. One such
tombstone marker is for Abraham Hunt, a merchant who assisted Washington during the Battle of Trenton. This burial ground predates the Revolutionary War.

52. The replacement marker "erected by a descendant, 1929" for
Mahlon Stacey (d. 1704), an early Quaker settler and judge in Trenton.
Riverview Cemetery, Trenton.

61 🐾 *Riverview Cemetery,* Laylor and Lamberton Streets, Trenton.
Thousands of early citizens were buried here in this lovely parklike location near the Delaware River. The earliest grave is marked by a plaque
placed there in 1929 by a descendant of Mahlon Stacey, who died in 1705.
Many Victorian-style marble monuments engraved with interesting symbols, as well as some red sandstone markers, are found throughout the
grounds.

Middlesex County

62 🐾 *First Presbyterian Burial Ground*
Cranbury
1734

Directions: From Exit 8A of the New Jersey Turnpike, turn right onto Route 32
and go to first traffic light. Turn left onto Route 535 west and proceed for about five
miles, following signs to Cranbury. Cross Route 130 and proceed into the town of
Cranbury. While on Main Street, look for the church and burial grounds on your
right, across from the historic Cranbury Inn Restaurant.

Nestled in this lovely historic village is the well-maintained Presbyterian
Burial Ground containing gravemarkers predating the Revolutionary War
period. Back then, the village was known as Cranberrytown and was host
to such well-known dignitaries as Washington, Lafayette, and Hamilton,
who visited Cranbury while their troops were stationed nearby just before
the Battle of Monmouth. Cranbury was noted for being a stagecoach stop,
and in 1804 Aaron Burr stayed here in his flight from Weehawkin, New
Jersey, to Philadelphia, after wounding Alexander Hamilton in the fatal
duel. The town has kept its uniqueness since those days, still maintaining
a colonial atmosphere. The church, Cranbury Inn, and numerous other
homes and businesses date from the 1700s and 1800s. Developers and
neon signs have not been allowed to ruin the quaint atmosphere.

Several hundred tombstones are in the First Presbyterian Burial
Ground, the oldest ones being to the right of the church. A nearby plaque
marks the many graves of soldiers, placed there by the Daughters of the
American Revolution in 1934. They include names such as Biggs, Stillwell,
Conover, Wyckoff, Snedeker, Newell, Applegate, Barclay, and Dey.

One of the most interesting inscriptions on a granite marker at Presbyterian tells a sad story of overland travel in colonial times:

> William Christie native of Scotland,
> late merchant of Philadelphia who
> was cut down in the flower of his Youth
> by falling from the Stage-coach
> near Cranberrey on the 14th of
> October 1796 and was killed on the spot.

A surprised-looking angel effigy with wings is carved on the unsigned sandstone marker of Ann Patten, who died September 18, 1762, at age thirty-five. Her lovely epitaph reads:

53. The quaint epitaph on this marker tells the sad tale of a young Scottish merchant from Philadelphia who fell from a stagecoach near Cranbury (spelled "Cranberrey" by the stonecarver) in 1796.

> Here lies that true & Loveing bride
> Who lived belovd Lamented died
> Who Now is gon we hope to rest
> Amongst ye Angels & ye Just

A marker signed "H. Osborne/Woodbridge" is for a church elder, Humphrey Mount, who died in 1801. Kissing doves appear above the delicate initials "H M." The epitaph gives a warning to readers:

> From this cold bed of humid clay
> Reader to you I cry
> Your time is short make no delay
> Prepare Prepare to die

The sandstone marker of Margaret Schanch, who died in 1794 at age fifty-eight, is clearly signed by a stonecutter. It is inscribed: "Cut by Aaron Ross, N Brunswick." The same lettering appears on the unsigned tombstone of Lydia Mount, who died in 1795. If you examine the letters "C" and "I," and the slant of the overall inscriptions, it becomes obvious that they were carved by the same person.

These are just a few of the many interesting markers dating from the late 1700s and early 1800s (see fig. 20). The family names of the interred match some of the names of streets and businesses in this historic town.

Planning your visit: The grounds are open to the public during daylight hours. Street parking is available. For more information, contact the church at (609) 395-0897, or the Cranbury Museum at (609) 655-3736.

63 ❧ *St. Peter's Episcopal Church Cemetery*
   Spotswood
   1757

Directions: From the New Jersey Turnpike, take Exit 9 and proceed on Route 18 south for about five miles. From Route 18, take the Main Street/Spotswood exit. Follow Main Street to the center of Spotswood (about two miles) and look for the church on your left. Enter the parking lot off Main Street or turn left onto DeVoe Avenue and take the road on your left into the burial grounds.

Spotswood was known as "Tory Territory" back in the Revolutionary War days, as many of the early settlers held allegiance to Great Britain. Named for the town of "Spotteswood" in Scotland, it was settled in the late 1600s. Some of these early settlers came from England, Scotland, Wales, and Ireland, as is noticeable when you read the last names on the tombstones. The tombstones are on the sides of a hill leading up to the Gothic-style church. St. Peter's history dates from 1757, when it received a charter from William Franklin, the last royal governor of New Jersey.

Running along the back of the church is a swiftly moving creek leading to nearby DeVoe Lake. Statuesque trees, surrounding the tall church spire rising high above the community, complete the picture. Years ago, the three closely spaced churches were referred to as "the Lord's side of the street," and the three taverns, on the other side, were known as the "Devil's side."

Several hundred tombstones of red and brown sandstone and white marble make up St. Peter's Cemetery. The earliest marker is a brownstone inscribed:

> Here lies the body of Andrew, son of
> Robert & Jane Campbell who
> departed this life the twentieth of
> November in year of our Lord one
> thousand and seven hundred and sixty Aged
> sixteen years, two months and 20 days

Of interest are the tombstones carved by Henry Osborne of Woodbridge. One of these markers is signed, but several others have sunk into the ground, obscuring any signature that may be present. The Osborne style is unmistakable: the stone is rounded at the top, with scalloped edges and a vinelike border and flowery initials carved at the top. The inscription on the signed stone reads:

> Cut by Henry Osborne, Woodbridge
> MW [in flowery italics]
> In Memory of Martilla Daughter
> of John Jolly & Wife of Peter
> Wilmut who deceased
> June 3 1793 Aged 49 years

There is also a stylized tulip at the top of the Mary Dorsat marker near the front of the church, dating from 1783. This is most likely a stone carved by an Osborne stonecutter.

Another interesting sandstone marker tells of the ethnic origin of the interred:

John Lewis
a native of Wales, Great
Britain, died May 3rd, 1843
aged 61 years, wife Hester died
Nov 11, 1846, aged 49 1/2 years
erected as a small tribute of
filial affection

On the right side of the church lie some undated fieldstone markers, one with the simple initials, M-M.

Scattered throughout the burial grounds are markers containing family names such as Applegate, Arnold, Appleby, Burgess, Carroll, Chapman, Cozzens, DeVoe, Kinnan, Murray, McLaughlin, Outcalt, and Stout. Some of their descendants still live in the community and throughout New Jersey. Many early settlers fled from Spotswood during the Revolutionary

54. A small, undated sandstone marker, St. Peter's Episcopal Church Cemetery, Spotswood. The two initials, "M-M," offer no clue as to who is buried below, but the marker is a good example of an early small headstone or footstone.

War because of their allegiance to Great Britain. The American patriots seized the iron, forge, and flour mills during the war, and the Tory owners and sympathizers fled. Some returned after the war, and others never returned, having settled elsewhere.

For more information concerning tombstone inscriptions, contact the church. All of the stones have been inscribed and placed on a map by a volunteer. A copy, dating from 1962, is also available at the Alexander Library Archives at Rutgers University.

Planning your visit: The burial grounds are well-maintained and very accessible to the public. For further information, contact the church directly at (908) 251-2449.

64 ?? *First Presbyterian Church Burial Ground*
   Woodbridge
   1690

Directions: From Route 1, take the Green Street exit east to Rahway Avenue. Turn left onto Rahway Avenue. The church and burial grounds are two blocks up on your right.

This shaded, peaceful burial ground seems to be incompatible with the noisy vibrations of the trucks and cars hurtling past on Route 35 to busy Route 9 or the Garden State Parkway. In this triangular-shaped lot are about five thousand burial sites, the oldest headstone simply saying "Feb 24, 1690 E.F.B." The older brownstone gravemarkers are depicted with angel or skeleton effigies. Some of the angel effigies appear to be distinctively male or female, even in their facial characteristics. The typical round-faced cherub with wings is ever present, as is the death's head with its grim expression.

The epitaphs found on the gravemarkers are most interesting and poetic, as is the case in the marker of Samuel C. Harriot, nine-year-old son of Samuel and Abigail Harriot, who died suddenly on July 22, 1808:

> Death like an overflowing stream
> Sweeps away our life, a dream
> An empty tale, a mourning flower
> Cut down and withered in an hour.

The gravemarker of Mary Cutter reads as follows:

> Here lies the body of Mary, wife
> of Samuel Cutter, who departed
> this life April 2, 1786 age 40
> years 6 months 4 days
> Weep not for me my friends
> For why my race is run
> It is the will of God
> And let his will be done.

The somewhat cynical epitaph of James Smith, who died October 18, 1772, at age seventy-two, reads:

> Farewell Vain World
> I've had enough
> I'm not grown
> Careless what thou

The first non-Indian child born in Woodbridge was Mary Compton Campbell, daughter of William and Mary Compton, born in 1667. She is buried in this churchyard. Family names that are prominent here include the Cutters, Barrons, FitzRandolphs, Pralls, and Bloomfields.

Dr. Moses Bloomfield lived in Woodbridge during the Revolutionary War and practiced medicine. He is buried in the Presbyterian grounds and is remembered for his antislavery position. At one time he personally owned fourteen slaves but gave them their freedom amid a speech and ceremony on July 4, 1783. Some of the former slaves chose to stay on as paid employees.

A number of tombstones in this burial ground were carved by Henry Osborne and date from the late 1700s to early 1800s. Osborne's gravemarkers have a distinctive soul effigy with puffy cheeks and braided hair. As you walk through the grounds, it is easy to spot his gravemarkers signed "H. Osborne Woodbridge."

Planning your visit: The grounds are open to visitors during daylight hours. Park in the lot in front of the church. For further information, contact the church at (908) 634-1024; they will most likely refer you to the cemetery superintendent. He is very knowledgeable about the tombstones and is accustomed to school groups and visitors touring

55. Note the distinctive tulip motif and elegant lettering on this stone for Thomas Brown (d. 1784, age eight). First Presbyterian Church Burial Ground, Woodbridge.

the grounds. Also visit nearby Trinity Church, with markers dating to the 1700s.

Other Notable Burial Grounds in Middlesex County

65 🙰 *St. James Episcopal Churchyard,* Woodbridge Avenue, Edison. Several hundred tombstones are located here and in the old Baptist Cemetery behind St. James, with nice sandstone markers from the 1700s. Find the no-longer-readable flat tombstone marker with crude lettering dating from 1693. This marker tells the story of twin boys who skipped church one day to gather mushrooms. The epitaph tells how they were "poyseend." Also to be seen here is the sandstone marker of Martha Pettinger, who died in 1729, with an early-style skull and crossbones.

66 ⚛ *Stelton Baptist Churchyard,* Plainfield Avenue, Edison.
Hundreds of tombstones from the mid-1700s, many old sandstone markers of the area's earliest settlers, the Drakes, FitzRandolphs, and others associated with the Piscataway Plantations are located here. Many of the sandstone markers have death's heads and soul effigies. Note the wonderful marker of Abraham Van Gilder, born on the high seas and died in 1818 at age 116! The earliest marker is that of Captain Andrew Drake, who died in 1743; the marker has unique old-style lettering and a soul-effigy design.

67 ⚛ *First Presbyterian Church Cemetery,* Main Street, Metuchen.
This cemetery is hidden behind a wooded area on Main Street. It can be easily spotted by the thousands of passengers traveling the trains daily, as it borders the train tracks. Some sandstone tombstones date from the late 1700s and are of early settlers with last names such as Kelly, Ayres, Shotwell, Ross, and Bloodgood. Some have DAR markers indicating the dead had fought in the Revolutionary War. Look for the gravemarker that seems to be growing out of a tree trunk. Park at the train parking lot and walk to the cemetery to view these gravestones.

68 ⚛ *Christ Episcopal Churchyard,* Paterson and Neilson Streets, New Brunswick.
This church is set in a historic area surrounded by new development in New Brunswick. It contains interesting sandstone tombstones dating back to pre–Revolutionary War times. Wonderful epitaphs and death's head

56. A unique motif of a serpent biting its tail, on the marker for John Downey (d. 1768, age thirty-eight). Christ Episcopal Churchyard, New Brunswick.

examples abound. Note the unique serpent and crossbones design on the sandstone marker for John Downey, who died in 1766.

69 ⱥ First Reformed Church Cemetery, Bayard and Neilson Streets,
    New Brunswick.

Early Dutch settlers formed this congregation back in the 1700s, making it New Brunswick's oldest church. Sandstone tombstones date back to 1746 and are surrounded by a wrought-iron fence. There are clear representations of death's heads and soul effigies on the tombstones, and some fieldstones. There are also some unusually large, white tombstones and several Revolutionary War stones.

70 ⱥ Van Liew Cemetery, Georges Avenue and Pine Street,
    North Brunswick.

Thousands of graves are in Van Liew Cemetery, which is still in use. An area in the back is for Jewish burials. The original grounds date from the

57. This may be one of the oldest extant markers in the state. The horizontal sandstone slab marker with skull, crossbones, and hourglass is for Helen Gordon (d. 1687, age twenty-seven) and four of her six children. In 1875 it was moved from an old cemetery on State Street in Perth Amboy to St. Peter's Episcopal Church Burial Ground, Perth Amboy.

58. The marble marker at St. Peter's Episcopal Church Burial Ground,
Perth Amboy, for Thomas Mundy Peterson and his wife, Daphne Peterson.
Peterson was the first black man to vote under the Fifteenth Amendment
to the United States Constitution.

1600s, though the earliest readable marker (Zuricher-style, no signature) is inscribed in Dutch, and is for Johannes Van Harlingen, who died in 1768. The marker of Richard Jacques, who died in 1792, resembles the Osborne stonecarver style. Near the Pine Street entrance are 519 reinterments of bodies and markers from the First Presbyterian Church in New Brunswick, which were done in the early twentieth century. The removal was a major undertaking, and careful records were kept of names and dates, from 1785 to 1909. The remains and stones were removed to make room for a new Sunday school, chapel, and recreation building. The stones are in a horizontal position and barely readable. In some cases, the grass has grown over part of the inscriptions.

71 ≈ St. Peter's Episcopal Church Burial Ground, Rector and Gordon
      Streets, Perth Amboy.
This is the oldest Episcopal church in the state, dating from 1722. From the grounds one has a view across the Arthur Kill to Staten Island. Many old sandstone tombstones mark the graves of early settlers from Scotland. The oldest readable marker is a flat sandstone for Helen Gordon, who died at age twenty-seven in 1687; it contains a nice epitaph and skull and crossbones design. Some markers are signed by Ebenezer Price. An interesting urn-style marker dating from 1773 on a flat sandstone can be found on top of the hill. To the right of the church on the bottom of the hill is the marker for Thomas Mundy Peterson, the first black man in the United States to vote under the Fifteenth Amendment.

Monmouth County

72 ≈ Presbyterian Burial Grounds
      Middletown
      1694

Directions: From the Garden State Parkway, take Exit 114, the Holmdel/Middletown exit. Proceed east on Red Hill Road for about two miles until it intersects with King's Highway. Make a right turn onto King's Highway and proceed about three quarters of a mile to the burial grounds at the corner of King's Court and King's Highway.

The earliest records tell of Dutch traders settling in Middletown in 1626. By 1664 about fifty persons of Dutch and English descent had settled in Middletown. When they died, these early settlers were buried on family estates or in the Presbyterian Burial Grounds. Dating back to 1684, this is one of the earliest burial grounds of European settlers in New Jersey.

At first view, the location of the Presbyterian Burial Grounds may surprise you. Rather than being the typical landscaped cemetery with a few trees scattered here and there, this cemetery is located in a dense thicket of large hemlock trees. A wooden fence runs along the front, and an informational plaque and sign are in front of the fence. Yet this small quarter-acre site of about fifty headstones is easy to miss, as the trees, shrubs, and underbrush hide it well. Directly behind the woods and grounds is a suburban neighborhood. A homeowner's adjacent garden shed serves as a boundary line, as there is no fence along the back of the grounds. Fourteen of the fifty headstones are in the section called the Hendrickson Burial Ground, which is separated by a split-rail fence from the remaining burial area. The Hendrickson family were early English settlers in the area, and their tombstones are made from marble, of simple rectangular or headboard design. A few of the markers have footstones. Epitaphs appear on several of the stones, but are difficult to read as they have sunk into the ground or become worn away over the years.

Early records tell of a simple log church built on the Presbyterian grounds in 1706. Hessian troops burned the log church in their destructive march down King's Highway in 1777, during the Revolutionary War. Deep in the woods, old wooden timbers are present, but their origin is unknown.

The oldest known gravestone at Presbyterian is the unusual marker for Captain John Bowne, an ancestor of Abraham Lincoln, who arrived in Middletown in 1663 after leaving Massachusetts because of religious persecution. He became a founder of Middletown's Baptist Church, which is now across the road. His marker is a little difficult to read—he died March 13, 1715 or 1716. Another marker is for John Bowne, Esq., who died in 1774. This gravestone is a slate color, of very large headboard style, and has rosettes carved in the top corners, and a three-dimensional cherub with wings on the sides. It is not like any other stone material or design found in New Jersey, and was probably imported from England. The stonecarver is thought to be an Englishman, William Valentine (see Welch 1987).

59. The gravestone of John Bowne, Esq. (d. 1774), is unique in its material and design. It is thought to have been carved in England by William Valentine and then shipped to New Jersey. Presbyterian Burial Grounds, Middletown.

A poetic epitaph is written on the headstone of Harry Leonard's wife, Caty, who died August 24, 1783, at age twenty-four:

> Here lies Quiet free from Life's Distracting Care,
> A tender Wife a freend sinceer—
> Whom death cut downe in Prime of Life you see,
> But stop my Grief we Soon Shall Equal be,
> And when the Lord thinks fit to End my time,
> With her beloved Dust I Mingle Mine.

The unknown stonecarver used a sad soul effigy with wings on both sides of the face; the eyes are almond shaped and cast slightly downward, topped by eyebrows and tiny strands of hair on top of the head (fig. 1).

Another graceful design appears on top of the headstone of Catherine Norrss Crookshank, who died in 1776 at age thirty-nine. The design consists of a rounded face with circular hair spirals on top, round eyes with large pupils, and a long nose. Under the epitaph is the signature of the well-known New York/New Jersey stonecarver John Zuricher.

60. Rubbings of distinctive angel head and rosette motifs as well as the signature of New York "stonecutter" John Zuricher on the gravestone of Catherine Norrss Crookshank (d. 1776, age thirty-nine).
(Courtesy Emily Wasserman, *Gravestone Designs, Rubbings, and Photographs from Early New York and New Jersey,* New York: Dover Publications, 1972.)

Here in Soft Peace for Ever Rest
Soft as ye Love, That Filled thy Breast
Let Hory Faith, Crown the Urn
And all ye Watchfull, Muses Mourn
Ye Messenger, which JESUS sends
To Call us to ye Sky,
For Ever there his Saints Do Dwell,
Beyond ye Rage, of Death and Hell.

Indian raids were common in early Middletown days, and during such times persons sought shelter in the town blockade that stood at the corner of King's Highway and Church Street. In 1721 a woman seeking shelter from a rumored Indian attack went into labor. Twin girls were born in this blockade and appropriately named Hope and Deliverance. Today, Hope's gravestone is in the Presbyterian Burial Grounds and reads: "Hope, wife of John Burrowes, died Oct 27th, 1792 in the 71st year of her age."

Relatives of the well-known early Dutch settler Penelope Van Princis Stout are known to be interred at the Presbyterian Burial Grounds. Penelope, born in the Netherlands in 1602, came to America with her husband, who was killed by the Indians in the Navesink Woods. They wounded Penelope and left her to die. She was later rescued by the Indians, went on to marry an Englishman, Richard Stout, and lived to age 110. Four members of the Stout family are buried at Presbyterian Burial Grounds. One of these interesting double sandstone markers is for John and Peggy Stout, two descendants of Richard and Penelope Stout. It says:

> In Memory of John, Son of Richard Stout Esq,
> departed this life August 16, 1783 aged 81 years 7
> months. Also Peggy, Daughter of Joseph and Jane
> Stout, died August 27, 1787 aged 3 months 5 days.

The actual burial site of Penelope Stout has never been determined, though it is assumed she was buried in one of the many burial spots of Middletown.

Planning your visit: Since this burial site may be overrun with brush and poison ivy, dress accordingly. Recent cleanup efforts by the local Eagle Scouts and the replacement of the wooden rail fence have improved its appearance. For further information contact the Middletown Historical Society at (908) 291-8739. Burial records can also be found at the Monmouth County Historical Association in Freehold.

73   *Old Tennent Church Cemetery*
Tennent
1731

Directions: From Route 9 just north of Freehold take Route 522 west to Tennent Road (Route 3). Turn right onto Tennent Road. The cemetery and church are on a hill directly to your right, next to Monmouth Battlefield State Park.

The burial grounds are surrounded by a wrought-iron fence and in a picturesque country setting. Near the front gate a historic marker tells us:

> Tennent Church—Erected 1751, this famous church was the pastorate of Reverend William Tennent. It stands on the famous Battlefield of Monmouth.

The burial grounds began with the purchase of one acre of land in 1731 from William Kerr, a local Scotsman. The congregation was also begun in

1731, when it moved from the Old Scots Church in Marlboro (see cemetery number 76). A temporary building was erected at that time. The earliest known burial took place in 1733, though there may have been earlier interments.

At one time, two graceful white oak trees towered over the burial grounds. Today only one of these trees remains, and it is said to be at least two hundred years old. Cannons and military artillery are on site, as the Battle of Monmouth was fought in the surrounding area in 1778. The church was even used as a hospital for wounded patriot soldiers: blood-stains still remain on some of the pews inside the church.

The oldest remaining tombstone is that of Benjamin Disbrow, who died in 1733 at age 63 (see fig. 14). His sandstone marker depicts a death's head and corresponding rectangular teeth, symbols commonly used at the time. Another marker representing other members of the Disbrow family is right next to the one of Benjamin Disbrow. The tombstone marking the burial of Susanne, wife of John Disbrow, and her five-month-old child, who died in 1739, has the same style lettering and gravemarker. Unfortu-

61. An early marker for Susanna Disbrow at Old Tennent Church Cemetery, Tennent. It lies next to two other Disbrow markers (see fig. 14) but is missing its top.

nately, the death's head portion on top has been completely removed for unknown reasons. A later death's head with a crown appears on the sandstone marker of Jonathan Forman, who died in 1784.

Look for the oldest markers around the boundaries of the church, except for the burial inside the church. The Reverend William Tennent, pastor of the church for forty-three years, was buried under the central aisle of Tennent Church. This was considered a great honor and not uncommon in colonial times.

The names on the headstones reveal a variety of ethnic backgrounds, such as French Huguenot, Dutch, and English, besides the Scots who started the congregation. The tombstone style and names have changed over the years to reflect new populations and stylistic changes in the surroundings. Many large Victorian-style monuments were erected at Tennent during the 1800s and early 1900s. The burial grounds are still in use today.

Tennent Church and grounds were widely photographed during the 1800s. The Trenton photographer Luther R. Cheeseman took a series of twelve prints that were made into a stereo card series (Moss 1971). They are considered to be of exceptional quality. It is interesting to note that few changes have taken place over the more than 125 years from the 1860s to now. The old-fashioned-looking mourners in the picture seem anachronistic to Tennent Church, which looks today as it did in the 1700s (see fig. 2).

Planning your visit: The burial grounds are open to the public. It is interesting to walk through them because of the historic gravemarkers and events that took place during the Battle of Monmouth. To see the inside of the church, call for an appointment at (908) 446-6299.

74 ❧ *Christ Church Burial Ground*
Shrewsbury
1769

Directions: From the Garden State Parkway, take Exit 109. Turn left or follow Route 520 west after the toll booths. Follow 520 all the way to Route 35, or Broad

Street. Turn right onto Broad Street and continue until it intersects with Sycamore Avenue. Christ Church and the burial grounds will be on your left.

The immediate area around Christ Church was originally a trail for the Lenni Lenape Indians, known as the Minisink, and ran from Freehold to the Atlantic Ocean. Today, Sycamore Avenue has replaced the old trail, with its tall hundred-year-old sycamore and buttonwood trees towering over the area. The trees also surround the church at this busy intersection, where a sign on Route 35 tells us:

> Christ Church-Converts of George Keith, 1702, became the nucleus of Episcopalian Congregation incorporated in 1738. This edifice was built in 1769.

Early members of this congregation had strong ties to England: note the iron crown at the very top of the church steeple. Among the first converts mentioned in the above plaque was William Leeds, a reformed pirate from Captain Kidd's crew. He left his estate to Christ Church in Middletown and to this church. Leeds is buried here, next to the tower on the north side of the church. His sea chest is occasionally exhibited by the church. Another item of interest is the Vinegar Bible, printed in 1717, and one of only eight copies in existence. During the Revolutionary War the patriots tried to destroy the church for its known Loyalist allegiance. It was even set on fire but saved by a nearby Quaker who witnessed the action.

A walk through the burial grounds at Christ Church will reveal hundreds of gravemarkers, old and new, as the churchyard is still in use. The tombstones date all the way back to the 1740s. Many sandstone markers contain the death's head and the grim epitaphs that were so common to that time. An example:

> Here lies interr'd the Body of
> Joseph Throckmorton who departed this life August
> the sixth in the year of our Lord one thousand
> seven hundred & fifty nine Aged
> Sixty five years Eleven months
> and twenty two days

A grim death's head appears on the brown sandstone marker of James Rusel. The rectangular rows of teeth are under the skull, with

62. Early death's-head marker for James Rusel (d. 1761, age forty-three).
Note the triangular nose and circular eyes typical on markers made by an
unknown stonecarver whose work can be found elsewhere in the
Christ Church Burial Ground, Shrewsbury.

wings on both sides. This marker is by an unknown stonecarver and is a good example of the death's-head style of that time.

A plain brown sandstone and simple epitaph appear for a woman identified as the second wife of William Green:

> In memory of MARY
> second wife of William Green
> who departed this life
> September the 1st 1802
> in the 45th year of her age
> As a testimony of regard this stone is erected.

Near the brick walkway in the burial grounds is an unusual occurrence of a cherry tree growing around a marker dating from the 1800s. The tombstone seems to be growing out of its trunk, splitting the tree in two.

This cemetery is very well maintained and will interest any visitor wanting to view a chronology of tombstone history. The gravemarkers begin with the Puritan symbolism, move on to the Victorian age, and end with the simplistic markers characteristic of the twentieth century.

Planning your visit: The burial grounds are open during daylight hours. The church offers tours by appointment; call (908) 741-2220. The church is at the intersection with the Allen House, built in 1667, Friends Meeting House, and the Shrewsbury Historical Society. This historic area was once part of the King's Highway, and is worth exploring by history buffs.

Other Notable Burial Grounds in Monmouth County

75 ❧ Old Brick Reformed Church Cemetery, Route 520 next to
Marlboro State Hospital, Marlboro.

This site was chosen by Dutch settlers from Long Island in 1699. The red sandstone markers have a variety of death's heads and angel effigies dating from the 1700s. Some of the names one can find here are Conover, Schank, Hendrickson, and DuBois.

76 ❧ Old Scots Burial Ground, Gordon's Corner Road, Marlboro.

These grounds date back to 1692 and today border a housing development, woods, and Gordon's Corner Road. This site of several acres has a

63. A wonderfully detailed sandstone marker for John Hendricks (d. 1760, age twenty-three). Old Brick Reformed Church Cemetery, Marlboro. Note the treatment of the hair on the soul's head.

monument in the center as its focal point, erected by the Scotch-Irish Society of America in 1889 as a memorial to early founders: Elder Walter Kerr, John Hampton, Jedidiah Andrews, and Francis Makemie. Note the brick crypt of the Reverend John Tennent, founder of nearby Tennent Church. His flat sandstone marker dates from 1732, with a double set of crossbones under the epitaph. The twin-skull effigies of William and Margaret Redford, carved by an unknown stonecutter in 1729, are fascinating.

77 ❧ *Old Topanemus Burying Ground,* between Topanemus Road,
near Route 18, Marlboro. Look for sign.

This site was originally the Quaker meetinghouse burial ground, and then the Episcopalian church burial ground, and dates from the early 1700s. Topanemus has many interesting tombstones of red sandstone carved into symbols of death's heads and angel effigies. Some Scottish names can be found on the stones: Reid and Reed family members, Loyd, Franses, and Warne. Read the inscription for Colonel John Anderson, born in Scotland and died in Manalapan in 1736.

64. Very large death's head with a triangular nose on the marker for Richard Clark (d. 1733). Old Scots Burial Ground, Marlboro.

78 ☙ *Mount Pleasant Cemetery,* on Route 516 near Route 79, Matawan. Alongside a busy road is this burial ground surrounded by an old-fashioned white picket fence. It dates back to 1763 and contains several hundred markers under large oak and sycamore trees. Most tombstones are from the 1800s, but a substantial number of red sandstone markers are from the 1700s. A few tall marble monuments and crude fieldstone markers are here as well. Note the large granite marker for Dr. Peter LeConte, who died in 1766. A differently-styled double-angel effigy design is on the marker for Helenah Forman, who died in 1783. Carved by an unknown stonecutter, the angel wings appear under the two angel effigies, rather than on the sides.

79 ☙ *Baptist Church Burial Ground,* King's Highway, Middletown. One of the first Baptist groups in New Jersey formed here in 1688, with settlers from Rhode Island. The Presbyterian grounds across the street were at first used for the Baptist congregation as well, until the Baptists

65. A pair of cherubs with collars and down-swept wings on the marker for Helenah Forman (d. 1783). Mount Pleasant Cemetery, Matawan.

started their own next to the church. There are about five hundred graves here, mostly with white marble markers of simple designs. Some of the most common names are Frost, Conover, Stout, Schenck, and Murray.

80 ❧ *Christ Episcopal Burial Ground,* King's Highway, Middletown.
Referred to as Old First Church, this group organized in 1688. William Leeds, a pirate with Captain Kidd, left money to this church to make amends for his piratical deeds. The burial ground contains mostly white marble markers dating from the 1700s. Read the interesting epitaph of Thomas Arrowsmith, who died in 1800. Some other names of early settlers buried here are Taylor, Stout, Frost, Willet, and Hendrickson.

81 ❧ *Reformed Church Burial Ground,* King's Highway, Middletown.
Across from the covered bridge are the old and new churches and the burial grounds. Take the circular driveway all the way around to the wooded area, where the tombstones can be found. Here are about fifty sandstone markers dating from the 1700s and white marble markers with old Dutch names such as Schenck and Henderson.

Southern New Jersey

Ocean

82 Barnegat—Sea Captain's Cemetery
83 Barnegat—Friends Meeting House Burial Ground
84 Lakewood—Greenwood Cemetery
85 Lanoka Harbor—Good Luck (Potter's) Churchyard
86 Toms River—Methodist Cemetery
87 Warren Grove—Warren Grove Cemetery

Burlington

88 Crosswicks—Crosswicks Friends Burial Ground
89 Burlington—Friends Meetinghouse Burial Ground
90 Burlington—St. Mary's Episcopal Church Burial Ground
91 Cookstown—African Methodist Burial Ground
92 Crosswicks—Orthodox Friends Burial Ground
93 Mt. Laurel—Jacob's Chapel African Methodist Burial Ground

Camden

94 Haddonfield—Friends Meetinghouse and Burial Ground
95 Camden—Harleigh Cemetery
96 Camden—Johnson Cemetery
97 Collingswood—Friends Burying Ground
98 Lawnside—Mt. Pisgah African Methodist Burial Ground

Gloucester

99 Swedesboro—Trinity Episcopal Church Burial Ground
100 Woodbury—Friends Meeting House and Burial Ground
101 Woodbury—Gloucester County Historical Society Library
102 Glassboro—Manahath Cemetery
103 Glassboro—St. Thomas Episcopal Church Cemetery
104 Mullica Hill—Quaker Meetinghouse Burial Ground

Salem

105 Daretown—Pittsgrove Presbyterian Church Burial Ground
106 Churchtown—St. George's Churchyard
107 Fort Mott—Finn's Point National Cemetery
108 Friesburg—Friesburg Lutheran Church
109 Quinton—Smith Burial Ground
110 Salem—Friends Burying Ground
111 Salem—First United Methodist Church
112 Alliance—Alliance Cemetery

Cumberland

113 Greenwich—Old Presbyterian Church Burial Ground
114 Bridgeton—Old Broad Street Church
115 Deerfield—Deerfield Presbyterian Churchyard
116 Roadstown—Cohansey Baptist Church Cemetery

Cape May

117 Cold Spring—Cold Spring Presbyterian Churchyard
118 Cape May Court House—Baptist Burying Ground
119 Cape May Court House—Fairview Methodist/Hand Burial Ground
120 Marmora—Trinity Methodist Church Burial Ground
121 Middle Township—Holmes Family Burial Ground
122 Palermo—Second Cape May Baptist Churchyard
123 Seaville—Seaville Methodist Churchyard

Atlantic

124 Head of River—Head of the River Cemetery
125 Mays Landing—Westcott Free Burying Ground
126 Pleasant Mills—Methodist Church Burial Ground
127 Smithville—Old Meetinghouse Burial Ground

Southern New Jersey

Ocean County

Directions: From the Garden State Parkway, take Exit 67 to Route 554 east, also known as West Bay Avenue. The Sea Captain's Cemetery, also known as the Old Masonic Cemetery, is about a mile up the road on your left. The Friends Meeting House can be reached by continuing on West Bay Avenue toward the ocean, across Route 9, where West Bay becomes East Bay.

Life for early settlers in Barnegat was linked closely to the ocean. Generations of shipbuilders and sea captains, salt workers, and even pirates began settling here in the 1720s. Barnegat was originally known as "Berendegat," whose Dutch origin meant "the place of breakers." Before the early Dutch settlers arrived, native American Indians lived in Barnegat for the summer months, to escape the heat inland.

Turning into the Sea Captain's Cemetery on West Bay Avenue, you will notice numerous white marble headstones of sea captains indicating their final resting places. Captains Inman, Soper, Birdsall, Woodmansee, Collins, Leeds, and Ridgeway are among those buried in this plot of several acres. The sea captain graves are easily found because the tombstones contain the title "Captain" before the surname. Sometimes the stones are embellished with symbols of the sea such as an anchor or a ship. One such tombstone (with a ship) says simply:

Homeward Bound
Isaiah
Son of Abram & Sarah J. Fort
died April 3, 1879 aged 24 years 2 mos & 21 days

Lee [stonecarver]

This is a most interesting cemetery to walk through, not only because of the number of sea captains in it but also because of the many
family plots surrounded by wrought-iron fences or displaying simple
markers. Many of the families represented here still use the plots for burials, reflecting descendants of four and five generations, some dating back
one hundred fifty years.

From the Sea Captain's Cemetery, be sure to proceed down West Bay
Avenue across Route 9 to the Friends Meeting House and Burial Ground.

66. Nautical symbols, an
anchor and buoy, adorn the
gravestone of Captain Thomas
Woodmansee (d. 1880), Sea
Captain's Cemetery, Barnegat.

67. A flying dove symbolizes the premature death of five-year-old John Nelson Inman (d. 1861), Sea Captain's Cemetery, Barnegat.

Surrounded by large red cedar trees, this plain meetinghouse dates from 1767. The graves date from 1759, though no markers can be found inscribed as such. As was customary among early Quakers, gravemarkers from before 1824 were not inscribed, making it impossible to tell who is buried in some sites. But it is known that the following Quaker names are represented in this burial ground: Birdsall, Cranmer, Collins, Weaker, Stokes, among others. The burial ground was also used for the many shipwrecked victims of ocean disasters. At one time, the meetinghouse was the only place of worship for miles around.

Planning your visit: Both burial grounds are open during daylight hours and are not enclosed. More information concerning both grounds can be found in the Barnegat Historical Society Heritage Center just up the road from the meetinghouse on East Bay Avenue. The Heritage Center contains information about the genealogy of the area's families and a history of the Barnegat area. Six historic buildings from the 1700s and 1800s can be found.

Other Notable Burial Grounds in Ocean County

84 ⭑ Greenwood Cemetery, Cedar Bridge Road, Lakewood.
This cemetery was once part of Woodlawn Cemetery in Lakewood. A very interesting section was set aside for the black cooks and maids who worked at the many shore resorts in the 1800s. Also of interest are the folk-art types of markers, including small metal signs used to mark graves.

85 ⭑ Good Luck (Potter's) Churchyard, Route 9 and Haines Street,
      Lanoka Harbor.
The Old Potter Church has a fascinating history: Thomas Potter built this church in 1760 to fill the need for a group that welcomed all denominations. It became known as the first Universalist group in America, with the

68. The Potter Meeting House, first built in 1770 and rebuilt in 1841, became the first Universalist church in America. One of the early religious founders, Thomas Potter (d. 1806), is buried behind the house. Good Luck (Potter's) Churchyard, Lanoka Harbor. (Undated postcard, early 1900s. Author's collection.)

69. Funeral urn and shroud symbols are common on markers from the 1700s and 1800s. This large, Victorian-era gravestone is for Anthony Parker (d. 1854). The inscription ends with the grim motto: *Memento Mori* (Remember Death). Good Luck Churchyard, Lanoka Harbor.

Reverend John Murray as its first minister. The churchyard is in a very serene setting, with wrought-iron benches, cedar trees, and a few hundred limestone and marble markers. Behind the green wrought-iron fence is the gravesite of Thomas Potter. Next door are campgrounds, used each July for an annual pilgrimage of Universalist church members.

86 ₰ *Methodist Cemetery*, Washington and Hooper Avenues, Toms River. This burial ground is notable for the white marble and limestone gravemarkers constructed for early sailors and sea captains, including Timothy Thompson and Captain William Giberson. An interesting marker identifies a Danish sailor, Christian Empson, who was shipwrecked nearby in the early 1800s. He remained in the area, became a prominent businessman, and married a colonist, Lydia Potter.

87 🞜 ***Warren Grove Cemetery,*** near Routes 72 and 539, two miles south on 539, Warren Grove. Look for sign.

Once a thriving town called Cedar Grove and Reevestown, it is now in the middle of nowhere. The cemetery contains about two hundred markers surrounded by pine trees. Many of the markers are simple fieldstones, others white limestone with inscriptions dating from the 1700s and 1800s. Some of the names on the stones are the same names found in towns all over South Jersey: Cranmer (Cramer), Brown, Reeves, Collins, Brewer, and others.

Burlington County

88 🞜 *Crosswicks Friends Burial Ground*
Crosswicks
1773

Directions: From Interstate 195 or Route 130 south of Trenton, exit at Route 524 east leading to Yardville. Proceed through Yardville and in the outskirts look for a sign on your right for Crosswicks-Hamilton Road. Turn right and follow this road for about two miles into Crosswicks. Follow Main Street through town and look for the meetinghouse just after a rather sharp turn; it will be on your right. Turn onto Church Street to access the driveway, which will lead you right up to the side of the meetinghouse.

Tall sycamore and oak trees surround this area, which was first used as a burial ground in 1691. This predates the two-story brick meetinghouse, built in 1773.

At first glance it will not be clear where the Friends Burial Ground is: there are so few markers that you must look closely to find them. If you stand within twenty feet and face the meetinghouse, you will see a small marble marker about six inches high and rectangular in shape. This marker is one of the oldest to be found in the county. It marks the grave of Mary Woodward, daughter of Anthony and Hannah Woodward, who died January 13, 1686, at an unknown age. The stone simply reads "Woodward," but early church records mention this as the first burial and give details concerning the interred. A footstone with a "W" on it lies a few feet away from the Woodward marker. Assuming the footmarker is Mary's, it would indicate that she was a small child, as the distance between the headstone and footstone is just several feet. A few other crude fieldstones are in the same general area, but none have inscriptions. If you look closely, you will find another small marble marker marking the burial of Lucy Thorn. It is barely readable, and has no date. The founder of Crosswicks, Thomas Foulkes, was buried here in 1714 at age ninety, but the precise location has never been found.

Crosswicks Friends currently have plans to mark the burial ground with one large marker to represent the many graves of early settlers that have no markers.

Crosswicks Meetinghouse is still used by the Friends, and is recognized as a historical site. For instance, in 1778 the meetinghouse was taken over by Hessian troops for use as a hospital and barracks. Later on, it was fired upon by cannons. Today, a cannonball remains in the wall, cemented in place to show visitors proof of this event. After the Battle of Trenton, the patriots took over the house as their barracks. It was a desirable shelter because it was one of the few that contained a stove for heating. Inside the meetinghouse is an Atsion stove, built in Atsion, New Jersey, from native bog iron. It is one of only three known such stoves to exist today; a framed letter next to it states that it was purchased in 1772. Another landmark at Crosswicks was an old oak tree that stood fifty feet away from the meetinghouse and had a circumference of seventeen feet. It had been there since at least 1682, but a windstorm felled it in 1975. A marker and lovely landscaped garden now stand in its place.

Planning your visit: The burial ground is open to the public during daylight hours. To see the meetinghouse, schedule an appointment by calling (609) 298-4362.

89   *Friends Meeting House Burial Grounds*
 Burlington
 1681

Directions: From the New Jersey Turnpike, take Exit 5 and proceed west on Route 541. This will become High Street. After you pass over the railroad tracks, look for the stone wall that surrounds the meetinghouse. It is at 222 High Street in Burlington.

In the downtown section of this quaint city of colonial buildings that have been converted into storefronts stands a thick stone wall with an iron gate.

If you swing open the heavy gate, you can get a closer look at the red brick meetinghouse, built in 1784. It is a lovely two-story structure with white pillars, oversized windows, and a porch extending the entire length. If you walk around to the back of the meetinghouse, you will find the oldest burial ground in Burlington County.

The simple white marble markers and crude fieldstones mark the graves of some early citizens of Burlington. Following Quaker tradition, there are few inscriptions on the stones, and only the most humble markers were used. It is known that the burial ground even predates the former meetinghouse, built in 1683. Friends records show that the large sycamore tree that is still present was already there when the great Indian chief Ockanickon was buried underneath it in 1681. His marker is a large rock containing a plaque given by the YMCA and YWCA campers of Camp Ockanickon in 1910. It reads:

> Near this spot lies the body of the
> Indian Chief Ockanickon, friend of the
> white man, whose last words were
> "Be plain and fair to all
> Both Indian and Christian
> As I have been."

70. The Indian chief Ockanickon was buried in 1681 beneath a sycamore tree in the Friends Meeting House Burial Ground, Burlington. He is commemorated by a stone marker and plaque presented by YMCA and YWCA campers of Camp Ockanickon in 1910.

Planning your visit: The meetinghouse grounds are generally kept open during daylight hours, but appointments are preferred. To visit the meetinghouse or other historical sites in Burlington, call (609) 386-3993.

90 & *St. Mary's Episcopal Church Burial Ground*
Burlington
1703

Directions: From the New Jersey Turnpike, take Exit 5 and proceed west on Route 541. Continue on 541 west about three miles into Burlington. Route 541 becomes High Street. Just past the railroad tracks look for West Broad Street. Turn left onto West Broad, and the burial ground and church are on the second block on the right side of the street.

Behind a stone fence and beneath many large trees lies one of the oldest burial grounds in South Jersey. St. Mary's Church dates from 1703, but the burial ground was in use as early as 1695. Today, two churches stand on this site, with thousands of gravemarkers placed close together.

The burial ground is filled with oak, sycamore, pine, and maple trees, some hundreds of years old. Animals include squirrels, rabbits, chipmunks, and birds, making St. Mary's look something like a wildlife sanctuary.

Most of the markers in the burial ground are composed of marble, light sandstone, or fieldstone. The oldest markers are in the area around the original church. Some of them are crude fieldstones that can no longer be read. The oldest inscribed tombstone is that of Mary Steward, who died in 1706 at age eighteen. Most of these older stones are white and of a simple design, with an urn shape or a round top. The inscriptions are barely legible on some of those dated prior to 1775.

The older St. Mary's Church, covered with stucco, has tombstones embedded into the walls of the church. They look quite fascinating and have vines growing over the bottom portions of the markers, which represent the persons buried under the church. This was a common and honorable practice in colonial times, frequently performed for former ministers and their families.

The cemetery contains tombstones of some famous men from colonial times: Elias Boudinot, first president of the American Bible Society; William Bradford, attorney general under George Washington; and Joseph Bloomfield, fourth governor of New Jersey, to name a few. These men

71. The gravestone of Rebecca McIlvaine (d. 1780?), one of several gravemarkers embedded in the stucco walls of Old St. Mary's Church, Burlington.

attended services at St. Mary's, as did other famous individuals such as George Washington, Captain James Lawrence ("Don't give up the ship"), and James Fenimore Cooper.

The block-long area that contains the two churches and the burial ground between them has been designated one of the national historic landmarks in Burlington. There are many other historic sites to visit, as the town has maintained many of its colonial landmarks.

Planning your visit: The burial ground is open to the public, and the newer church still holds services. Contact the church for an appointment to examine the interior of St. Mary's. Walking and bus tours of Burlington's historic district are available; call the Burlington County Historical Society for information at (609) 386-4773. The church is just on the edge of the historic sector; to see the rest continue north on Wood Street. Around the corner from St. Mary's are many homes dating from the colonial period.

Other Notable Burial Grounds in Burlington County

91 ❧ African Methodist Burial Ground, Main Street, Cookstown.
This early church built in 1839 is near McGuire Air Force Base. The burial ground dates from the late 1700s, and has simple white markers and assorted fieldstones.

92 ❧ Orthodox Friends Burial Ground, Ward Street, Crosswicks.
Behind the Chesterfield Township Historical Society is a traditional Quaker burial ground. The simple marble and fieldstone gravemarkers contain names and dates dating from the 1800s and are lined up in orderly rows.

93 ❧ Jacob's Chapel African Methodist Burial Ground, Church
Road, Mt. Laurel.
Here are early AME burials, dating from the underground railroad days in New Jersey. Buried in this churchyard is the celebrated "Doctor of the Pines," James Still, who died in 1882.

72. Behind the Chesterfield Township Historical Society are the orderly rows of graves of the Crosswicks Friends Burial Ground, Crosswicks, dating from the 1800s. This group left the original Crosswicks Friends Meeting on Church Street to form their own meeting after disagreements over doctrine could not be resolved.

Camden County

94 ❧ *Friends Meetinghouse and Burial Ground*
   Haddonfield
   1732

Directions: From Interstate 295 south near Camden, take Exit 34 to Route 70 west. Follow to Route 41 to Haddon Avenue. Proceed on Haddon into Haddonfield. Look for a sign and road on the left designating "Friends Meetinghouse," on the corner near the intersection of King's Highway and Friends Street.

As you park next to the meetinghouse, you will notice the burial ground across the road in a hilly, parklike setting. Typical of many Friends' grounds are the large sycamore and oak trees planted hundreds of years ago. These lofty trees seem to offer protection to the clusters of grave-markers scattered throughout the area. Surrounding the burial ground is a stone fence, partially formed from bricks of the former meetinghouse, built in the 1700s. Within this stone enclosure are the simple white marble gravestones and fieldstones of Haddonfield's earliest citizens: Evans, Tomlinson, Duffy, Estaugh, Richardson, and Gill, among others. Several hundred markers positioned on small mounds are scattered throughout the grassy area. As is traditional with Friends, simple initials and family names are used to mark the small tombstones. No epitaphs will be found on the gravestones, except for the plaque honoring Elizabeth Haddon, "The founder and proprietor of Haddonfield, born 1680 died 1762." The bronze plaque in the section of the burial ground that is across from the meetinghouse describes her as being "Remarkable for resolution, prudence and charity."

A romantic story tells how Elizabeth Haddon founded the settlement. It all began in London, England, in the Haddon household. The Haddons were Quakers who were deeply impressed by a young preacher named John Estaugh whom they met at a gathering in London. Mr. Haddon invited him to the family home for dinner that evening. It was there that his fourteen-year-old daughter Elizabeth met John. They became acquainted over the next four years when John visited Elizabeth's father. The two men would spend hours discussing their shared ideals concerning the Quakers, a religion not well accepted in London. Unaware of Elizabeth's love for him, John left England to preach the Friends' ideals in America.

73. A simple, white marble gravemarker in Friends Meetinghouse and Burial Ground, Haddonfield. This marker lacks even the usual initials to identify the person buried there.

Mr. Haddon had no sons, so he sent his daughter Elizabeth to begin a settlement in America. At age twenty, Elizabeth sailed for America to settle on 400 acres of land her father had purchased in East Jersey. This was an unusual endeavor for a lone woman in 1701, but Elizabeth was a very determined young person. John Estaugh and Elizabeth Haddon eventually met again. John was still unaware of Elizabeth's love for him, so she put aside her modesty and proposed to him. He accepted her marriage proposal and joined her settlement in Haddonfield. Their love story has been described in Henry Wadsworth Longfellow's "Theologian's Tale" in *Tales of a Wayside Inn*. Throughout their marriage, both John and Elizabeth were leaders of the Quakers, performing many services for the colony. The couple was responsible for setting aside a section of the burial ground for the poor. This section can be seen today, in the northwest corner of this beautiful setting.

Planning your visit: The burial ground is enclosed by an unlocked gate across from the meetinghouse. Allow some time to walk in the colonial area of Haddonfield on King's Highway and the surrounding area. Historic plaques mark many of the homes in town. For more information about the area, visit the Haddonfield Historical Society at 343 King's Highway.

Other Notable Burial Grounds in Camden County

95 ⁊ Harleigh Cemetery, Haddon Avenue and Vesper Boulevard, Camden.

The many acres in this burial ground contain thousands of markers dating from the 1800s. Harleigh became one of the first landscaped cemeteries in South Jersey. It contains many ornate Victorian-style tombstones, statues, and huge mausoleums in a hilly parklike setting. The most commonly visited gravesite is of the distinguished poet Walt Whitman. To find it, follow the sign directing you (to the left) when you enter from the front. The poet designed his own simple crypt and wrote his own epitaph: "For that of me which is to die."

96 ⁊ Johnson Cemetery, 38th and Federal Streets, Camden.

Here lie many African-Americans of the 1800s. The cemetery was neglected for years, so the stones are in rough shape. Some inscriptions point out the "Colored Regiments" of the United States. Note the gravesite of William Miles Butts, the first black policeman in Camden, who died in 1899.

97 ⁊ Friends Burying Ground, Eldridge Avenue, Collingswood.

Near the lake stands the only evidence of an early settlement and the first Quaker meetinghouse in the area, dating to 1681. The burial ground, with its simple white marble markers and fieldstones, dates from the late 1600s. The Sloan Burial Ground adjoins the Friends Cemetery. It was established in 1790, by James Sloan, after a disagreement with the Quakers. A marker reads: "Here is no distinction/Rich and poor meet together/The Lord is Maker of them all/by James Sloan, 1791."

98 ⁊ Mt. Pisgah African Methodist Burial Ground, Warwick and Mouldy Roads, Lawnside.

This church was originally referred to as the first African Methodist Church. It became a stop for the underground railroad during the 1800s. African-American war veterans are buried here.

Gloucester County

99 ❧ *Trinity Episcopal Church Burial Ground*
Swedesboro
1784

Directions: From the New Jersey Turnpike, take Exit 2 and proceed onto Route 322 west. After about one mile, turn left (south) onto King's Highway or Route 551; this will bring you right into Swedesboro. The burial ground is behind the church on King's Highway. Additional burial grounds can be found by turning right onto Church Street and going two blocks.

Swedesboro, formerly known as Raccoon, was settled by the Swedes in 1642. Sixty years later the Trinity Episcopal Church was founded on the same grounds that hold the present church. It became the first Swedish Lutheran church in New Jersey. Prior to this, the Swedish Lutherans had to cross the Delaware River to attend services in Wicacoa, now known as Philadelphia. This was an obvious hardship, so when an enthusiastic but unqualified minister, Lars Tollstadius, offered to found a church at Raccoon, the Swedes welcomed him with open arms. The Swedish church representative in America opposed this and asked him to leave the country. Tollstadius ignored orders, and became the resident minister of Trinity Church. In 1702 a simple log church was built, where Tollstadius reigned for four controversial years. At one time he was involved in a scandal with a young woman in the community, and before he could be tried by a jury, his body was found floating in the Delaware River. No one could explain whether he was murdered or committed suicide, and it is not known where he was buried.

Today, the log-cabin church founded by Lars Tollstadius has become a two-story brick building with "1784" inscribed near the top. The church has a burial ground in the back shaded by maple, buttonwood, and cedar trees. The burial grounds two blocks away are surrounded by a low brick wall with an unlocked iron gate.

The tombstones in both churchyards number several thousand and are made from white marble or sandstone. Most of the markers have simple rounded tops or urn-shaped stones. Many have become slanted or have sunk into the ground over the years. Some are of Revolutionary War

74. Hundreds of Swedesboro's eighteenth-century Swedish settlers are buried in
a grassy field two blocks away from Trinity Episcopal Church Burial Ground.

soldiers, as both British and American soldiers used the church and parsonage during the war. Mad Anthony Wayne even stayed overnight one
cold night in February 1778, arriving late with three hundred men. He just
missed the British commander, who arrived the next morning to capture
General Wayne. The entire area was filled with soldiers for the duration
of the war, as were many other regions of New Jersey along King's Highway. Some of the more well-known soldiers buried in the grounds were
Colonel Boddo Otto, Colonel Thomas Heston, Colonel Robert Brown, and
Captain John Daniels. Most of the other names found in the burial grounds
are of Swedish or English descent, as the church became a Protestant
Episcopal Church in the late 1700s.

The oldest remaining marker in the graveyard is behind the church
in the thirteenth row. It is the barely readable marker of Samuel Linch, who
died at age fifty-eight in 1763. The next row behind the Linch marker contains an inscription of a typical saga in colonial life, when people frequently died in their prime:

Sarah Tittermary, wife of
Richard Tittermary of the City of
Philadelphia d 25 Sep 1793
aged 40 yrs & 5 mos who left a
husband & 8 children

Some of the stones at Trinity are not readable or are simple field-stones, but all have been copied in a list available at the Gloucester County Historical Society in Woodbury.

Planning your visit: The burial grounds behind Trinity and two blocks away on Church Street are open to the public during daylight hours. To visit the inside of the church, call (609) 467-1227; a tour is available. The church still holds Sunday morning services.

100 ᨀ *Friends Meeting House and Burial Ground*
Woodbury
1696

Directions: From the New Jersey Turnpike, take Exit 3 to Route 168 south and then to 130 south. Turn right onto North Broad Street and proceed two blocks to the meetinghouse at 124 North Broad Street.

The Quakers built the meetinghouse on this hill in Woodbury in 1715. Today it remains one of the most attractive sites in town, surrounded by ancient elm and buttonwood trees. Prickly-pear cactus can also be found throughout the area, including in the burial grounds. Here are markers of some of Woodbury's earliest citizens. The two-story traditional meeting-house is of red brick with a wide porch across the front and several entrances. Visitors are welcome to come inside the building, which contains the original unpainted woodwork from 1715. This meetinghouse was the battleground headquarters of the British troops during the Revolutionary War. Lord Cornwallis and his troops occupied it in 1777. Later on, the Americans used it as their headquarters. The adjacent burial ground was acquired in 1696, and contains some undated and illegible fieldstone markers, presumably from these early years.

This cemetery is the burial site of members of the Wood family, who had left their homes in England and come to America for religious free-

75. The very weathered marker for Mary Wood (dates illegible), one of the twenty-one Wood family members whose gravemarkers and remains were moved to higher ground in Woodbury's Friends Meetinghouse and Burial Ground. Other markers and bodies were swept away when the Woodbury Creek flooded the old burial ground.

dom. Richard Wood and his family established the community of Woodbury back in 1681 near the Woodbury Creek, about two miles from the grounds. Crude fieldstones marked these early graves. One stone had the initials "RW," thought to have been Richard Wood. In the mid-1800s, when the banks of Woodbury Creek overflowed, some of the bodies and markers floated away. Until the early 1950s the partially submerged burying ground was in danger of disappearing. In 1951 the Superior Court of New Jersey determined that the remains of the twenty-one people buried there should be moved to higher ground. They were reinterred in Woodbury Friends Burial Ground, and a granite monument was placed near the rows of Wood family members.

Henry Wood's granddaughter, Ann, became a legend in New Jersey history. Ann was married to James Whitall. She was a devout Quaker and heroine of the Battle of Red Bank, fought nearby in 1777. During the war, George Washington decided to build Fort Mercer in part of Whitall's apple orchard. Ann Whitall was encouraged to leave before the battle began, but refused, saying she could be useful later on. As the battle raged around her home, she calmly stayed indoors, working on her spinning wheel. Even when a cannonball flew in through the window and lodged itself into the wall next to her, she calmly retreated to the cellar for the remainder of the battle. Afterward, she made herself useful by tending the wounded soldiers in her home, both British and American. While tending Count von Donop, a wounded British commander, she scolded him for coming to America and fighting the patriots. He died later and was buried between the Whitall home and Fort Mercer.

Both Ann and her husband were buried in the meetinghouse burial grounds. Their plain white markers say: "Ann Whitall, died September 22, 1797, aged 82"; and "James Whitall, died September 29, 1808, aged 92." A complete list of burials is available at the Gloucester County Historical Society Museum just blocks away at 58 North Broad Street.

Planning your visit: The burial ground is open to the public. Turn in the driveway from busy North Broad Street and park behind the meetinghouse. If you would like to visit inside the meetinghouse, services are at 11:15 Sunday mornings, or call for an appointment at (609) 845-5080. If you continue down Broad Street and turn onto Hessian Avenue, you can visit the Whitall House, Red Bank Park, and the battleground monument (call 609-853-5120).

Other Notable Burial Grounds in Gloucester County

101 ❧ *Gloucester County Historical Society & Library,* 17 Hunter Street, Woodbury.

This is not a burial ground, but it is notable for currently housing burial stones from construction sites in the county. They are unceremoniously propped up against the back of the building for safekeeping. It is not known where the remains are. Some markers appear to be primitive folk-art lettering and style; a few even date up through the 1900s. It is thought that some are from the Mantua Creek area.

102 ❧ *Manahath Cemetery,* Main Street and Delsea Drive, Glassboro.

Manahath is still in use and is said to contain many early unmarked graves. There are a few 1800s tombstones of white sandstone and marble in a lovely parklike setting. Read William Smith's epitaph, a tribute to a man in

76. Two headstones from the fifty salvaged by workers at construction sites and fields in Gloucester County. They now lean against the sides of the Gloucester County Historical Society building. The location of the remains is unknown.

deep pain: "In sore affliction he bore his pain. Till God did call him home." Manahath is Hebrew for "resting place."

103 🍂 *St. Thomas Episcopal Church Cemetery,* Main and Focer Streets, Glassboro.

Here is a Gothic-style native sandstone church among lovely buttonwood and hemlock trees. The surrounding burial grounds date from 1791, with the oldest white marble markers found in back of the church. An interesting Victorian-style tree-trunk marker stands on the right side of the church.

104 🍂 *Quaker Meetinghouse Burial Ground,* Main Street, Mullica Hill.

The meetinghouse and burial grounds in this early Finnish and Quaker settlement date from 1806. Many Quaker soldiers who fought in the Civil War are buried here. Quakers were usually pacifists, but these soldiers had felt strongly about antislavery issues.

Salem County

105 ❧ *Pittsgrove Presbyterian Church Burial Ground*
Daretown
1767

Directions: From the New Jersey Turnpike, take Exit 2 to Route 322 east to Mullica Hill. Go through the town and follow signs for Route 77 south. Continue on 77 south for about ten miles to Pole Tavern. Daretown is two miles from Pole Tavern; the church and burial ground are on your left.

This church and surrounding area has been declared a historic site by the New Jersey Register. Restoration work makes this a particularly interesting area to visit. A log cabin has been rebuilt in the back of the church to show the original meetinghouse that was erected in 1740. A brick path leads back to the cabin, surrounded by sycamore and oak trees. A bench is along a path, and a nearby trickling stream completes the pastoral countryside setting. The two-story church, which was rebuilt with many of the original bricks, is in the front of the site. If you look closely, you can find carved initials from early congregation members on some of the bricks. Over the huge oak doors is the following inscription:

     N G   Nehemiah Greenman
     V D M Verbi dei Minister (minister of the word of God)
     1767
     P G C Piles Grove Church

Beginning in 1770, the church became known as Pittsgrove rather than Pilesgrove, in honor of William Pitt, the English statesman respected by the colonists.

The burial ground contains about a thousand markers of early settlers in the area, including twenty-six Revolutionary War soldiers. Most of these early settlers came from Long Island, New York, or East Jersey. They were of various ethnic and religious backgrounds such as French Huguenot, Dutch Reformed, and Scotch or English Presbyterian. Their tombstones are made from white sandstone, marble, or granite. The designs are simple, with slightly rounded or urn-shaped tops and occasional footstones. The inscriptions on the stones are simple and straightforward. In the front is the marker of Colonel Samuel Hunt, who served in both the

77. A postcard from the early 1900s picturing the old (foreground) and new (background) Pittsgrove Presbyterian Church Burial Ground, Daretown.

French and Indian War and the Revolutionary War. Another soldier's marker reads:

Louis DuBois
1755 – 1823
With Washington
at Valley Forge

Another reads:

Ruillier Steven native of Guadelupe
died March 7, 1802
age 15-1-0

A walk through the area will show many names of early settlers in the area such as Auld, Wood, Newkirk, Burt, Eedwell, and Dare. The settlers first arrived in this area and built homes around 1700; the earliest burials at Pittsgrove are from the 1750s. Look for the markers of Mary Moore, who died January 14, 1754, aged seventy years, and the tombstone of Nathaniel Whitacar, who died in 1753 at age fifty-eight.

Planning your visit: The burial ground is open to the public and is not enclosed. Also visit the Baptist Burial Grounds a half mile away on the left, and the Dare and Cook Houses. Both date from 1700. The Dare House was the home and store of Samuel Dare, for whom the town was named. You will have passed both of these sites on your way into town from Pole Tavern.

Each year at Christmas, the church draws many visitors for a special service, when organists play two pipe organs for the crowds of people. For more information about this service or a tour of the church, call (609) 358-8439.

Other Notable Burial Grounds in Salem County

106 ✒ *St. George's Churchyard,* Route 49 just south of Interstate 295, Churchtown.

This is the site of a Swedish Lutheran Church and burial ground dating back to 1714. The earliest stones are from the late 1700s: white sandstone markers with urn-style tops. Interesting epitaphs can be found, such as on the Thomas Weber tombstone, which tells us he is "not dead, only sleeping" and urges us to "prepare for death and follow me."

107 ✒ *Finn's Point National Cemetery,* off Route 49, Fort Mott.

The area is full of fascinating historical accounts, as there are thousands of Civil War soldiers buried here. The Confederate soldiers were kept prisoner in nearby Fort Delaware and Pea Patch Island during 1863, and they were not treated properly by the Union soldiers. Thousands died from disease and brutal treatment and were buried at Finn's Point. Today there are both Union and Confederate monuments to honor the Civil War soldiers buried here. Markers to honor Spanish-American and German war prisoners of World War II can also be found here. Be sure to read all the moving, poetic plaques throughout the cemetery and note the stately Norway and silver maples, planted in the 1870s.

108 ✒ *Friesburg Lutheran Church Cemetery,* Remsterville Road, Friesburg.

This is one of the oldest Lutheran churches in New Jersey. The church and burial grounds date from 1726. Some stones are inscribed in German and most are simple white marble markers.

109 🕏 *Smith Burial Ground,* Route 45, north of Quinton.
A monument was erected here to honor the many American soldiers killed during the skirmish at Quinton on March 18, 1778. It has been designated a National Cemetery. The nearby Captain William Smith House dates from 1700 and sequestered the British soldiers during the ambush.

110 🕏 *Friends Burying Ground,* West Broadway, Salem.
The Quaker meetinghouse was built in 1681. Many burials took place here, but in observance of Quaker rules, no markers were used until 1824. The tall, majestic oak tree known as the "Salem Oak" is thought to be around four hundred years old and shades the entire front part of the burial ground.

111 🕏 *First United Methodist Church,* Walnut Street, Salem.
Here is the tombstone for Benjamin Abbott, famous Methodist preacher, who had strong persuasive powers and obtained many converts. He is

78. In a country setting just west of Vineland is the Alliance Cemetery, notable for containing early burials of Eastern European Jewish immigrants who moved from New York City to resettle in this area.

buried on the right side of the church; his grave has a plain white marker
with a lengthy epitaph.

112 ❧ **Alliance Cemetery,** off Route 540, on Gershel Avenue, Alliance.
This burial ground conveys a history of the early settlements of the
Hebrew Immigrant Society in New York City in the 1880s. Russian and
Polish Jews were resettled here in the nearby planned communities such
as Alliance, Brotmanville, Carmel, and Rosenhayn. The cemetery is on
about ten acres.

Cumberland County

113 ❧ Old Presbyterian Church Burial Ground
Greenwich
1717

Directions: From Bridgeton, take Route 49 west to Shiloh. Turn left and continue
through Roadstown and on to Greenwich. The church is about eight miles from
Shiloh, on Greate Street, just north of the historic area.

Greenwich was once the largest town in Cumberland County, and was
known as a major transportation center in colonial times. Situated on the
Cohansey River, it was also the official port of entry for all ships traveling
on the Delaware River. Greenwich remained important until the mid-
1700s, when roads became more widely used in the county and the town
of Bridgeton was chosen as the county seat, putting an end to any further
significant growth in Greenwich.

Today, the town still maintains its colonial appearance along Greate
Street, with its two-mile stretch of homes dating back to the seventeenth
and eighteenth centuries. Tourists have not yet discovered this quaint
town, which is one of its great appeals. There are no billboards, no
modern homes, stores, or condos that are normal for a typical New Jersey
town of the 1990s. If you continue down Greate Street, you will approach
an area around the burial ground with large elm trees, which were

79. Many headstones are stacked in back of Greenwich's Old Presbyterian Church Burial Ground, waiting to be placed in an upright position.

planted years ago from seeds brought to Greenwich from the Boston Commons elms.

The burial ground and Old Presbyterian Church are about half a mile north of the town's historic area. The first church was built of simple logs around 1707, across the street from the location of the present-day red brick church. The log church and important church records were destroyed in a fire in 1739, and the new church was built in the 1800s. Greenwich Presbyterian Burial Ground is across the street from the church. This picturesque cemetery has a black wrought-iron fence in the front and is open on the sides. Over a hundred white marble markers and several rectangular brick vaults and marble monuments stand on this plot of several acres surrounded by mature trees. It is notable for containing the remains of four of the seven participants in Greenwich's own "Boston Tea Party," which took place in 1774. During the tea boycott, a British sea captain stored his tea in a loyalist's basement in Greenwich. Similar to the events at the Boston Tea Party, seven patriots dressed as Indians burned the tea and were later brought to trial. They were never convicted. These four buried here are Thomas Ewing, Joel Fithian, Joel Miller, and James B. Hunt. Their individual epitaphs are as follows:

Thomas Ewing Esq Surgeon and Practitioner of
Physic After having served his country with fidelity and
reputation in a variety of important offices Civil and
Military Died highly beloved and much lamented Oct 7 1782
In the 35th year of his age

Sacred to the memory of Joel Fithian who departed
this life November 9 1821 in the 71 year of his age
He was a soldier in the Revolution and served his
Country in many important offices and the Church in
Greenwich as a Ruling Elder with zeal and fidelity
Reader imitate his virtues that your end may like his be peaceful!

In memory of Joel Miller who died December 8, 1827
aged 80 years

In memory of James B Hunt who departed this life
Aug 5 1824 in the 71st year of his age
He served his country in her
struggle for Independence and
afterwards filled various Civil
offices with fidelity to the Public

A walk through the burial ground reveals that many early citizens lived to be over seventy years old. But all too often, many died in infancy or early childhood, and women died from complications in childbirth. The Maskell tombstones tell a sad story through their inscriptions. Mary Maskell died at age twenty-nine in August 1806, leaving behind four young children and her husband. Within the next two months, her husband, Abijah Maskell, died at age thirty-four, and three of her four children also died. Two of these children were her 20-day-old twin sons. There is no marker for the fourth child.

Another young mother died, soon after the birth of her third child, at age twenty-three. Her inscription reads:

80. Grave of Civil War veteran William Belford Ewing (d. 1862), Old Presbyterian Church Burial Ground, Greenwich. The epitaph explains how this young soldier was "taken sick in Virginia" and was "finally permitted to come home to die" at age twenty-five.

In memory of Mrs Sarah White the wife of John White merchant of Philadelphia and daughter of Alexander Moore and Sarah his wife who departed this life the 18th day of October 1770 a few days after the birth of her third child in the 23rd year of her age

She lived much desired and
Died much lamented
Inexorable death what beauty
hast thou effaced What expectation
hast thou cut short
Our souls would learn the heavenly art
To improve the hours we have
That we may act the wiser part
And live beyond the grave.

Many soldiers are buried at Greenwich, and to honor their veteran status small flags have been placed on their graves. One such grave contains a marker with an inscription for a Civil War soldier. It tells of William Belford Ewing, who died November 15, 1862, at age twenty-five. His epitaph appears on a white marble marker and reads:

> He served as a volunteer in the first New Jersey Cavalry for 14 months, was taken sick in Virginia, languished a long time in a Hospital and was finally permitted to come home to die.

How graceful and lovely is the youthful soldier's grave.

One of my favorite epitaphs still warns passersby. On the white marble, urn-shaped tombstone of Rachel Holmes, who died at age forty in 1789 and is buried next to her veteran husband, Colonel Abijah Holmes, is the inscription:

> Readers! Seek not the merit of this fair
> Upon the surface of unfeeling stone
> Ask of the honest heart its graven there
> Perhaps you'll find it written on your own.

Planning your visit: The burial ground is open to the public. Park along the side of the road or across the street in the church parking area. Be sure to visit the Cumberland Historic Society in the Gibbon House (1730). A tour of the town can be arranged by calling (609) 455-4055 or (609) 451-8454.

Other Notable Burial Grounds in Cumberland County

114 🕭 *Old Broad Street Church Cemetery,* Broad Street and West Avenue, Bridgeton.

The burial grounds date back to 1774. Located on about ten acres of land is the red brick church, surrounded by beautiful maple and cedar trees on a slight incline. Many of the tombstones are made from white marble and have inscriptions that are now difficult to read, the earliest dating from the late 1700s. Many of the Victorian-style markers from the 1800s carry interesting symbols. About three hundred noted soldiers and statesmen from the Revolutionary War are buried here, including high-ranking captains, majors, and a general, as well as a judge and senator.

81. The simple headstone for "Mary, Consort of John Rutan," praises her as "One of the best of mothers" and features a willow tree and monument design. Mary Rutan died in 1852, age seventy-six. Old Broad Street Church, Bridgeton.

115 ❧ *Deerfield Presbyterian Churchyard,* Deerfield Street, Deerfield. This village was settled in 1725, and the original log cabin church was built in 1732. The beautiful native sandstone church built in 1771 replaced the burned-down log cabin. In this burial ground are fieldstone, limestone, marble, and sandstone markers that date back to the 1700s. The early epitaphs reflect the Puritan background of the settlers.

116 ❧ *Cohansey Baptist Church Cemetery,* Roadstown. Between Greenwich and Route 49 are an old brick church and burial ground dating from the 1700s. The settlers buried here originally came from Tipperary County in Ireland and from Wales. Here are several hun-

82. Unfortunately a common sight in New Jersey: headstones toppled and cracked by vandals. Old Broad Street Church, Bridgeton.

83. The Deerfield Presbyterian Churchyard, as seen in an early twentieth-century postcard. Little has changed over the years. (Author's collection.)

dred tombstones made of white marble and fieldstone. Note the interesting crude fieldstone markers with partial inscriptions. Names of the buried include Ware, Watson, Sayre, and Bacon.

Cape May County

117 ❧ Cold Spring Presbyterian Burial Ground
Cold Spring
1714

Directions: From the end of the Garden State Parkway, turn west (right) onto Routes 9 and 109. Then make another right at the next traffic light onto Route 162. The church is on the right side of the road.

This burial ground contains the most tombstones of Mayflower descendants to be found in any one cemetery outside of Massachusetts. Many of these early descendants became whalers and plantation owners in Cape May County. Thirty-two families organized the Presbyterian Church in 1714 and built a small log cabin near what was known to be an Indian burial ground. The log cabin has long since disappeared; the current structure is the third church at Cold Spring. Today, some descendants from the original thirty-two families are still affiliated with Cold Spring Presbyterian, over 275 years later!

Some one thousand tombstone markers stand in Cold Spring, yet they don't represent all the burials. It is known that during the cholera epidemic of 1832, scores of victims were buried here at night, and no records or markers were left to identify them. The oldest gravestone is located on the side of the church and marks the grave of Sarah Spicer. It is a simple white marble marker with an urn-shaped top and its inscription is no longer legible. A similar replacement stone is next to the original, which reads:

In Memory of Sarah Spicer
Who died July
the 25 1742 Aged
65 years

84. An unusual depiction of the Resurrection—an angel at the empty sepulchre—carved on the gravestone for Lydia Leaming (d. 1836, age sixty-six). The inscription over the carving reads, "Thy spirit to Heaven ascends." Cold Spring Presbyterian Churchyard, Cold Spring.

Cemetery representatives say that several other Spicer family headstones can be found at Cold Spring, but they are known to be replacements for the lost or damaged original ones. Some original markers and remains never made it to this new location, as they were lost to the encroaching sea on the Spicer Plantation lands. This entire part of South Jersey has lost land due to the continual erosion of the shoreline.

An early Spicer replacement stone has this inscription:

Jacob Spicer, Esq
departed this Life Sept 17
1765
in the 49th year
If ought that's good or great could save
Spicer had never seen the Grave

Some of the names of early settlers found throughout the burial ground include Swain, Whilldin, Williamson, Ludlam, Smith, Crawford, Crowell, and Edwards. The Whilldins were descended from John Howland, one of the original Pilgrims from Plymouth, Massachusetts. Hundreds of Whilldin family descendants are buried in this cemetery, and others still live in South Jersey. One of the better-known descendants buried at Cold Spring is Edgar Page Stites, who wrote the well-known hymn "Beulah Land," in 1876.

Other settlers known to be buried at Cold Spring did not have a tombstone, or had unmarked fieldstone or red cedar markers. Most of these crude markers have disappeared over the years, but one of them can be seen in the cemetery office, where it is kept fastened to the wall for safekeeping. The name and date have been completely effaced by time.

Cold Spring Burial Ground has some interesting epitaphs. The following warning to onlookers is my favorite:

> In Memory of Thomas Buck,
> Who departed this life
> Febry 24th 1790
> Aged 46 years
> Mortals who chance to tread this sacred spot
> Look on my Tomb and read the human lot
> Your flesh like mine must reunite with clay
> To worlds unknown your spirit soars away
> Know me before and you must come behind
> Depart from hence and keep this thought in mind.

Planning your visit: The burial ground is open to the public. If the caretaker is available, ask for the leaflet describing the history of the burial ground and facts about the people buried here. For further information, contact the church at (609) 884-7351 or the nearby Cape May Historical and Genealogical Society at (609) 465-3535.

Other Notable Burial Grounds in Cape May County

118 ❧ *Baptist Burying Ground,* Church Road, off Route 9, Cape May
     Court House.
This burial ground consists of several acres and hundreds of tombstones. The markers are made of white marble and sandstone or crude fieldstone. Many markers are in family plots with stone marker partitions and iron bars. Some gravemarkers have smaller footstones with initials inscribed on them. Note the heaven symbolism on Sylvitha Iszard's marker.

119 ❧ *Fairview Methodist/Hand Burial Grounds,* Route 9, Cape May
     Court House.
This burial ground has hundreds of markers with interesting Victorian period designs and symbols. Especially noteworthy are the cradles for the Cresse twins, Captain Hand's ship, and the "fallen bouquet" of Annie Claypoole (see fig. 17).

85. This gravestone for Sylvitha Iszard (d. 1893) is striking for the directness of the hand symbol and the inscription, "Meet me in heaven." Baptist Burying Ground, Cape May Court House.

86. Twin headstones for Captain German Hand and his wife, Emma, can be found inside a wrought-iron fence in Cape May Court House and Burial Ground. Note the tops of the markers, which read "Our Father" and "Our Mother."

120 ❧ *Trinity Methodist Church Burial Ground,* now Seventh Day
Adventist, 20 North Shore Road (Route 9), Marmora.

There are hundreds of white marble markers from the 1800s and a few red
sandstone and fieldstone markers from 1700s; the earliest dates to 1759.
Also look for the sandstone marker of David Evans with a wonderful effigy
of a smiling angel with almond-shaped eyes. The stonecarvers' style is
unique to this part of New Jersey, suggesting the markers may have been
shipped here from New York or New England. (Also see fig. 88.)

121 ❧ *Holmes Family Burial Ground,* Route 9, opposite County
Historical Museum, Middle Township.

Just alongside Route 9 are about a dozen white marble markers and a brick
vault for members of the Holmes family. Be sure to read the "Honest Man"
epitaph written on the Robert Morris stone from 1789.

122 ❧ *Second Cape May Baptist Churchyard,* 600 South Shore Road
(Route 9), Palermo. The sign says Seaview Cemetery and is
directly across from the Baptist Church.

The older section is in the front, and the back section is still in use. The
oldest marker was made of sandstone for Amelia Stillwell, who died in

87. It is unusual to find a marker with this angel effigy and crown motif in
South Jersey: they are much more common in Central and North Jersey.
This sandstone marker for David Evans dates from 1759. Trinity Methodist
Church Burial Ground, Marmora.

1759. Among the many markers are prickly pear cactus growing wild throughout the grounds. The carving of the angel effigy appears to be the same as the ones found in the burial ground in Marmora. Note the unusual angel effigy with closed, downcast eyes on the sandstone marker of Nicolas Stillwell. Most markers here are made of marble; only a few are of red sandstone.

123 ❧ Seaville Methodist Churchyard, Route 9, Seaville.
Here are hundreds of gray marble markers from the 1800s next to an unusual Victorian-style church. Next to the church is a matching church birdhouse, as is common in many Victorian homes in Cape May. These picturesque grounds are surrounded by many cedar trees. The older stones are to the left of the church next to a plaque that tells about the Townsends, who were early settlers in Seaville. Read the sad epitaph of Reuben Townsend, who died in 1812 at age fourteen and is buried under a cedar tree (see page 38).

88. The unknown stonecutter of the gravestone for David Evans (see fig. 87) in Marmora also carved this angel effigy marker for Amelia Stillwell (d. 1759) in the Second Cape May Baptist Churchyard, Palermo. A prickly pear cactus is growing in front of the tombstone.

Atlantic County

124 ❧ *Head of the River and Baptist Cemeteries*
Head of River
1790

Directions: From the Garden State Parkway, take Exit 36 to Route 40 west. Continue on 40 west to the intersection with Route 50 in Mays Landing. Take 50 south to county road 666 (right turn), which will intersect with Route 49. The church and burial grounds are at the intersection of Routes 49 and 666.

The cemetery is in a remote forested area of New Jersey, but two hundred years ago it was part of a thriving colonial town. The Baptist and Methodist burial grounds are the only remainders of this once vital trade community along the Tuckahoe River. Back then, many visitors would have arrived by schooner or boat sailing down the Tuckahoe from the coast. Other visitors, such as the fiery Reverend Benjamin Abbott, who spoke at the dedication of Head of the River Methodist Church two hundred years ago, arrived on horseback. The town and church records show that Head of the

89. The Baptist Cemetery in Head of River, which contains only about ten headstones, has become part of the larger Methodist Head of the River Cemetery across the road.

90. The headboard-shaped gravemarker and pious epitaph for the Reverend Isaac Bonnel (d. 1794, age sixty-four), Baptist Cemetery, Head of River.

River reached its peak at about 1827, and in the years after became one of many South Jersey ghost towns. Now all that remains is the simple two-story church and surrounding cemetery.

Head of the River Cemetery contains about a thousand markers made mostly of marble, white sandstone, and granite, as well as a few fieldstones. The Baptist burial ground is separated from the Methodist by Route 666. Next to the Baptist grounds is a large sign, explaining that the cemetery was founded in 1790 and is now considered part of the Head of the River Cemetery. The Baptist grounds have only about ten tombstones. One of these is the urn-shaped sandstone marker of the Reverend Isaac Bonnel, who died in 1794 at age sixty-four. A religious epitaph appropriate for a man of his occupation is on his marker. Another minister, Peter Corson, was buried at Head of River, and his marble marker tells how he died May 31, 1797, at age twenty-three years and five months. His epitaph reads simply:

> He Preach'd the Gospel of the Lord
> And is gone home to his Reward.

Peter Corson's tombstone is signed by I. Hay, whose hometown is unknown. Another stonecutter signed himself as "T. Cox—Vineland."

The Methodist grounds across the way have markers of eight Revolutionary War soldiers. Flags or DAR symbols have been placed next to them to designate their veteran status. The tombstone of Joseph C. Estell, who served with General Lafayette, has a flag next to it. The marker is a lovely blend of white marble with an urn-shaped top.

Here are some glowing tributes to several women who died young and were buried at Head of the River:

> In memory of Mary Gandy, relict of
> Uriah Gandy
> who departed this life
> Feby 4th 1826 aged 21
> years 3 months & 15 days
> Her married months were only few
> Before she bid her friends adieu
> Beneath this raised ruef she lies
> Till Gabril's trump shall bid her rise.

Another sad tribute is inscribed for Esther Townsend, who died at age twenty-five on March 14, 1825:

> Like as a bud nipt off the tree
> So death has parted you and me.

These are only a few of the interesting epitaphs to be found in this country cemetery. This part of New Jersey is noted for attracting migratory birds, which can be plainly seen and heard in the cemetery.

Planning your visit: The burial grounds are open to the public during daylight hours and are well maintained. An annual dedication ceremony is still held here, as the graveyard has some fairly recent burials of descendants of the settlers. For information contact the Atlantic County Historical Society in Somers Point at (609) 927-5218.

Other Notable Burial Grounds in Atlantic County

125 ❧ *Westcott Free Burying Ground,* next to Presbyterian Church,
Cape May Avenue and Main Street, Mays Landing.
In the center of the historic part of town are about one hundred markers
of fieldstone, granite, and marble under oak trees hundreds of years old.
Of particular interest is the ornate Victorian-style gate and fence around
the Walker family plot. Also read the epitaph of Captain Nicholas Rape,
who died in 1832.

126 ❧ *Methodist Church Burial Ground,* Route 542, Pleasant Mills.
This is an interesting burial ground because of the iron tombstones to be
found here, along with the usual marble and sandstone markers. Batsto

91. The graceful headstone
for a baby, Sarah
Hollingshead (d. 1836, age
4 months and 2 days). In the
background is the iron
fence enclosing the Walker
family plot, Westcott Free
Burying Ground, Mays
Landing.

ironworks is close by and is thought to be the source of the iron used in the gravemarkers. Earliest burials were in the late 1700s, when this was a small colony. By now the town has nearly disappeared. Many persons buried at Pleasant Mills were Revolutionary War soldiers or seamen; be sure to read their epitaphs.

127 ❧ *Old Meetinghouse Burial Ground,* Moss Mill Road, Smithville. The cemetery and meetinghouse in this shore community date back to the early 1800s. The burial ground contains white limestone and marble markers and fieldstones. The names inscribed are of the earliest settlers in the area: Leeds, Clark, Conover, Doughty, among others. The epitaph of Ann Clark reads: "She has done what she could."

Appendix 1

Notable Burials
in New Jersey

Camden

Harleigh Cemetery, Haddon Avenue
    Walt Whitman (poet, *Leaves of Grass*)

Hillside

Evergreen Cemetery, N. Broad Street
    Mary Mapes Dodge (writer, *Hans Brinker*)
    Stephen Crane (writer, *The Red Badge of Courage*)
    Edward Stratemeyer (writer, *Bobbsey Twins series*)

Middletown

Mount Olivet Cemetery, Chapel Hill Road
    Vince Lombardi (sports)

Mount Laurel

Jacobs Chapel Cemetery
    James Still (black doctor of the Pines)

Newark

Fairmount Cemetery
    Clara Maas (nurse, combatted yellow fever)

Perth Amboy

St. Peter's Episcopal Church, Gordon Street
    Thomas Mundy (first black man to vote)

Princeton

Princeton Cemetery, Witherspoon and Wiggins Streets
 Grover Cleveland (former president of the United States)
 John O'Hara (writer, *Butterfield 8*)
 Aaron Burr (former vice president of the United States)
 John von Neumann (mathematician, cybernetics)

Trenton

Riverview Cemetery, Lalor and Lamberton Streets
 George McClellan (Civil War leader)
 John Roebling (architect, Brooklyn Bridge)

Old Friends Burial Ground, East Hanover and Montgomery Streets
 George Clymer (signer of the Declaration of Independence)

West Orange

Edison National Historic Site, Main Street and Lakeside (private estate, need permission to enter)
 Thomas Edison (scientist and inventor)

Appendix 2

Educational Activities

1. Compile a list of all surnames found in a burial ground. Place like names together in columns. Which family name was most frequently mentioned? What country was most likely its ancestry? Search the local phonebook to see if the surname is still represented in the area.

2. Search carefully near the bottom of the gravemarker and try to find a stonecutter's signature. Research your library to find information about the person and other localities where his stones can be found. What are the similarities in the stones?

3. Find the oldest gravemarker with readable dates in the burial ground. Copy everything carved on the stone, including the epitaph, if available.

4. What is the name and age of the youngest person buried in the cemetery? The oldest?

5. Check the years of death of the persons interred. Did more people die in any one year than in others? Could there have been an epidemic? A cold winter? A war? Use your local library to find out.

6. Take a grave rubbing of an interesting epitaph and design on a tombstone, if one is allowed to do so.

7. Sketch or take a photo of a gravemarker and find out the type of stone and style it represents.

8. Study the various types of stones used in the gravemarkers of a burial ground. Which stones appeared to weather better than others?

9. Draw a scale map of the graveyard, placing the stones in their correct positions on this smaller-scale map. Number each stone and make a list underneath the map for reference purposes. The list can include details such as who is buried there, date, and epitaph.

10. What are some common misspellings on the earlier gravemarkers? Are they consistent with a certain type of stone? Are the dates represented differently than they would be written today?

11. Describe the surroundings of the burial ground. Is it on level ground, near a body of water? What type of vegetation, plants, trees, or wildlife is present?

12. Take a random sample of ten tombstone dates and find the mean, median, and mode of the age at which the persons died.

13. Were there or are there any old buildings on the burial ground site? Are they presently being used? Are there any open spaces of land where a meetinghouse or church once stood?

14. Find out who is responsible for maintaining the grounds. Have there been any acts of vandalism in recent years?

Appendix 3

Cemetery Inventory Form

Name/address/phone number of recorder _____

Date recorded _____

Cemetery name(s) _____

Location _____
(sketch on back if more detail is needed)

Cemetery contact person _____

Address _____

Group or private ownership: _____
    City/town _____ County _____ State _____ Federal _____
    Church _____ Historical Society _____
    Other (explain) _____

Maintenance contact person _____

Overall Accessibility and Condition:
    Flat terrain _____ Wheelchair accessible _____
    Hilly terrain _____ Overgrown _____
    Need hiking boots/gloves _____

Gravemarkers:
    Approximate size _____
    Number of markers _____
    Burial date range _____

    Oldest marker _____ Most recent _____
    Material _____
    Ethnic origin of deceased _____

Other background information:

Appendix 4

Gravestone Form

Name of cemetery _____

Location _____

Name of recorder _____

Date _____

Type of gravestone _____
(headstone, footstone, box vault, etc.)

Material _____

Photo attached: _____ yes _____ no

Source of previously taken photo (book, collection) _____

Name of person interred _____

Date of death/age _____

Inscription: exactly how it is carved, line for line. Use letter X for
unreadable letters; continue on back if needed

_____

_____

_____

_____

General condition of gravestone _____

Noticeable repair work _____

Stonecarver information _____

Additional information (genealogical, historical, etc.)

_____

_____

Appendix 5
County Historical Resources

Atlantic County Historical Society
    907 Shore Road
    P.O. Box 301
    Somers Point, NJ 08244
    (609) 927-5218

Atlantic County Office of Cultural Affairs
    1333 Atlantic Avenue, 7th Floor
    Atlantic City, NJ 08401
    (609) 345-6700, ext. 2243

Bergen County Historical Society
    1209 Main Street
    Box 55 (Steuben House)
    River Edge, NJ 07661
    (201) 343-9492

Bergen County Division of Cultural and
Historic Affairs
    Administration Bldg., Court Plaza South
    21 Main Street
    Hackensack, NJ 07601-7000
    (201) 646-2786

Burlington County Historical Society
    457 High Street
    Burlington, NJ 08016
    (609) 386-4773

Burlington County Cultural and
Heritage Commission
    49 Rancocas Road
    Mount Holly, NJ 08060
    (609) 265-5068

Camden County Historical Society
    Park Blvd. & Euclid Avenue
    Camden, NJ 08103
    (609) 964-3333

Camden County Cultural and
Heritage Commission
    Hopkins House
    250 South Park Drive
    Haddon Township, NJ 08108
    (609) 858-0040

Cape May County Historical and
Genealogical Society
    DN 707
    Route 9
    Cape May Court House, NJ 08210
    (609) 465-3535

Cape May County Cultural and
Heritage Commission
    Library Office Bldg.
    DN 101
    14-34 Mechanic Street
    Cape May Court House, NJ 08210
    (609) 465-1005

Cumberland County Historical Society
    P.O. Box 16
    Greenwich, NJ 08323
    (609) 455-4055

Cumberland County Cultural and
Heritage Commission
    P.O. Box 969
    Vineland, NJ 08360
    (609) 692-9580

Essex County Division of Cultural and
Historic Affairs
   22 Fairview Avenue
   Cedar Grove, NJ 07009
   (201) 857-5290 or 5693

Gloucester County Historical Society
   17 Hunter Street (Library)
   P.O. Box 409
   Woodbury, NJ 08096
   (609) 845-4771

Gloucester County Cultural and
Heritage Commission
   Budd Boulevard Complex
   P.O. Box 337
   Woodbury, NJ 08906
   (609) 384-6950

Hudson County Division of
Cultural and Heritage Affairs
   114 Clifton Place
   Jersey City, NJ 07304
   (201) 915-1212

Hunterdon County Historical Society
   114 Main Street
   Flemington, NJ 08822
   (908) 782-1091

Hunterdon County Cultural and
Heritage Commission
   Administration Building
   Flemington, NJ 08822
   (908) 788-1256

Mercer County Cultural and
Heritage Commission
   640 S. Broad Street
   Trenton, NJ 08650
   (609) 989-6701

Middlesex County Cultural and
Heritage Commission
    Middlesex County Annex
    841 Georges Road
    North Brunswick, NJ 08902
    (908) 745-4489

Monmouth County Historical Association
    70 Court Street
    Freehold, NJ 07728
    (908) 462-1466

Monmouth County Historical Commission
    27 E. Main Street
    Freehold, NJ 07728
    (908) 431-7413

Morris County Historical Society
    Acorn Hall
    68 Morris Avenue
    Morristown, NJ 07960
    (201) 267-3465

Morris County Heritage Commission
    Morris County Courthouse
    P.O. Box 900
    Morristown, NJ 07960
    (201) 829-8117

Ocean County Historical Society
    26 Hadley Avenue
    Toms River, NJ 08753
    (908) 341-1880

Ocean County Cultural and
Heritage Commission
    38 Hadley Avenue
    Toms River, NJ 08753
    (908) 244-2121, ext. 2200

Passaic County Historical Society
Lambert Castle
Garret Mountain Reservation
Valley Road
Paterson, NJ 07503
(201) 881-2761

Passaic County Cultural and
Heritage Council
Passaic County College
College Boulevard
Paterson, NJ 07509
(201) 684-6555

Salem County Historical Society
79-83 Market Street
Salem, NJ 08079
(609) 935-5004

Somerset County Historical Society
P.O. Box 632
Somerville, NJ 08876
(908) 722-0018

Somerset County Cultural and
Heritage Commission
P.O. Box 3000
Somerville, NJ 08876
(908) 231-7110

Sussex County Historical Society
82 Main Street
Newton, NJ 07860
(201) 383-6010

Sussex County Arts and
Heritage Council
P.O. Box 275
Lafayette, NJ 07848
(201) 383-0027

Union County Historical Society
    116 E. 4th Avenue
    Roselle, NJ 07203
    (201) 245-9010

Union County Office of Cultural
and Heritage Affairs
    633 Pearl Street
    Elizabeth, NJ 07202
    (201) 558-2550

Warren County Historical and
Genealogical Society
    313 Mansfield Street
    P.O. Box 313
    Belvidere, NJ 07823
    (908) 475-4298

Warren County Cultural and
Heritage Commission
    Administration Bldg.
    Route 519
    Belvidere, NJ 07823
    (908) 475-6204

Appendix 6

Additional Sources

The Association for Gravestone Studies
  30 Elm Street
  Worcester, MA 01609
  (Quarterly journal, annual conferences; regional and national)

Genealogical Society of New Jersey
  P.O. Box 1291
  New Brunswick, NJ 08903
  (Monthly magazine)

The National Society of the Daughters of the American Revolution
  1776 D Street, NW
  Washington, DC 20006
  (Annual report; update on new findings of soldiers' graves)

New Jersey Graveyard Preservation Society
  P.O. Box 5
  East Brunswick, NJ 08816
  (Newsletter, programs)

New Jersey Historical Commission
  4 N. Broad Street
  CN-305
  Trenton, NJ 08625
  (General information)

New Jersey Historic Preservation Office
  501 E. State Street
  CN-404
  Trenton, NJ 08625
  (General information)

New Jersey Cemetery Board
    20 W. State Street
    CN-040
    Trenton, NJ 08625
    (Consumer complaints, legislation)

National Register of Historic Places
    National Park Service
    U.S. Department of the Interior
    P.O. Box 37127
    Washington, DC 20013-7127
    (Pamphlets; applications for historic site nominations)

Bibliography

Arbeiter, Joan, and Cirino, Linda. *Permanent Addresses*. New York: Evans Publishing Co., 1988.

Baugher, Sherene, and Winter, Frederick A. "Early American Gravestones: Archaeological Perspectives on Three Cemeteries of Old New York." *Archaeology* 36, 3 (1983): 46–53.

Beck, Henry Charlton. *The Jersey Midlands*. New Brunswick: Rutgers University Press, 1939.

Beck, Henry Charlton. *The Roads of Home*. New Brunswick: Rutgers University Press, 1956.

Beck, Henry Charlton. *More Forgotten Towns of Southern New Jersey*. New Brunswick: Rutgers University Press, 1963.

Benes, Peter. *The Masks of Orthodoxy: Folk Grave Stone Carving in Plymouth County, Mass*. Amherst: University of Massachusetts Press, 1977.

Burns, Stanley B. *Sleeping Beauty: Memorial Photography in America*. Altadena, Calif.: Twelvetrees Press, 1990.

Cohen, David Steven. *The Folklore and Folklife of New Jersey*. New Brunswick: Rutgers University Press, 1983.

Cohen, David Steven, and Williams, Lorraine E. *Pinelands Folklore*. New Brunswick: Rutgers University Press, 1987.

Conlon, David. "To the Potter's Field." *The New Yorker*, July 19, 1993, pp. 42–54.

Cottrell, Alden T. *The Story of Ringwood Manor*. The Ringwood Manor Advisory Committee, 1974.

Crowell, Elizabeth Ann. "Migratory Monuments and Missing Motifs: Archaeological Analysis of Mortuary Art in Cape May County, New Jersey, 1740–1810." Ph.D. diss., University of Pennsylvania. Ann Arbor, Mich.: University Microfilms, 1983.

Cushing, Thomas, and Sheppard, Charles E. *History of the Counties of Gloucester, Salem and Cumberland, New Jersey*. Philadelphia: J. P. Lippincott and Company, 1883.

Decker, Amelia Stickney. *That Ancient Trail: The Old Mine Road*. Trenton: Trenton Printing Company, 1942.

Deetz, James, and Dethlefsen, Edwin. "Death's Head Cherub, Urn and Willow." *Natural History* 76, 3 (1967): 28–37.

Derry, Ellis. *Old and Historic Churches of New Jersey.* Union City, N.J.: William H. Wise and Company, 1979.

Dickerson, Robert B., Jr. *Final Placement: A Guide to the Deaths, Funerals, and Burials of Notable Americans.* Alogonac, Mich.: Reference Publications, 1982.

Dorwart, Jeffrey M., and Mackey, Philip English. *Camden County, New Jersey, 1616–1976: A Narrative History.* Camden, N.J.: Camden County Cultural and Heritage Commission, 1976.

Duval, Francis, and Rigby, Ivan. *Early American Gravestone Art in Photographs.* New York: Dover Publications, 1977.

Ellis, Nancy, and Hayden, Parker. *Here Lies America.* New York: Hawthorn Books, Inc., 1978.

Elmer, Lucius. *History of the Early Settlement and Progress of Cumberland County, New Jersey.* Bridgeton, N.J.: 1869.

Forbes, Harriette Merrifield. *Gravestones of Early New England and the Men Who Made Them: 1653–1800.* New York: Da Capo Press, 1967.

Gillon, Edmund Vincent, Jr. *Early New England Gravestone Rubbings.* New York: Dover Publications, 1966.

Greenberg, Gail. *A Survey of Johnson Cemetery.* Camden, N.J.: Camden County Historical Society, 1978.

Griscom, Lloyd. *The Historic County of Burlington.* Mt. Holly, N.J.: Burlington County Cultural and Heritage Commission, 1973.

Hatcher, Patricia Law. *Abstracts of Graves of Revolutionary Patriots, vols. 1–4.* Dallas: Pioneer Heritage Press, 1987.

Heinlein, David A. "The New Brunswick–Japan Connection: A History." *The Journal of the Rutgers University Libraries,* vol. 52, no. 2, 1990.

Jackson, Kenneth T., and Vergara, Camilio Jose. *Silent Cities: The Evolution of the American Cemetery.* New York: Princeton Architectural Press, 1989.

Kingman, Bradford. *Epitaphs from Burial Hill.* Brookline, Mass.: New England Illustrated Publishing Company, 1892.

Koykka, Arthur S. *Project Remember: A National Index of Gravesites of Notable Americans.* Alogonac, Mich.: Reference Publications, 1986.

Kull, Andrew. *New England Cemeteries: A Collector's Guide.* Brattleboro: Stephen Greene Press, 1975.

Leigh, Freeman. *Historic Notes on Fairmount, New Jersey.* Bound Brook, N.J.: Tewksbury Publishers, 1982.

Ludwig, Allan I. *Graven Images: New England Stonecarving and Its Symbols, 1650–1815.* Middletown, Conn.: Wesleyan University Press, 1966.

McCormick, Richard. *New Jersey from Colony to State, 1609–1789.* Cedar Grove, N.J.: Rae Publishing Co., 1981.

McDowell, Peggy, and Meyer, Richard E. *The Revival Styles in American Memorial Art.* Bowling Green, Ohio: Bowling Green State University Popular Press, 1993.

McMahon, William. *South Jersey Towns, History and Legend.* New Brunswick: Rutgers University Press, 1973.

Mandeville, Ernest W. *The Story of Middletown.* Middletown, Conn.: Christ Church, 1927.

Marion, John Francis. *Famous and Curious Cemeteries*. New York: Crown Publishers, 1977.

Mellet, Dorothy W. *Gravestone Art of Rockland County*. Tappan, N.Y.: Hudson Valley Press, 1990.

Mellick, Andrew D., Jr. *The Old Farm*. New Brunswick: Rutgers University Press, 1948.

Meyer, Richard E. *Cemeteries and Gravemarkers: Voices of American Culture*. Ann Arbor, Mich.: University Microfilm International Research Press, 1989.

Meyer, Richard E. *Ethnicity and the American Cemetery*. Bowling Green, Ohio: Bowling Green University Popular Press, 1993.

Moss, George H. *Double Exposure: Early Stereography of Historic Monmouth County*. Sea Bright, N.J.: Plowshare Press, 1971.

Perinchief, Elizabeth M. *The History of Burlington County, N.J., 1687–1975*. Burlington, N.J.: Burlington Historical Society, 1975.

Pierce, Arthur D. *Smugglers Woods: Jaunts and Journeys in Colonial and Revolutionary New Jersey*. New Brunswick: Rutgers University Press, 1960.

Potter, Gail M. *Stories behind the Stones*. Cranbury, N.J.: A. S. Barnes, 1969.

Prouvel, George R. *The History of Camden County, New Jersey*. Philadelphia: L. J. Richards & Co., 1886.

Radko, Thomas R. *Discovering New Jersey*. New Brunswick: Rutgers University Press, 1982.

Raser, Edward J. *Morris County Burial Grounds Inventory*. Morristown, N.J.: Morris County Historical Sites Committee, 1975.

Rawson, Marion Nicholl. *Under the Blue Hills: Scotch Plains*. Plainfield, N.J.: N.J. Interstate Printing Company, 1974.

Sloane, David Charles. *The Last Great Necessity: Cemeteries in American History*. Baltimore: The Johns Hopkins University Press, 1991.

Smillie, James, and Walter, Cornelia. *Mount Auburn Illustrated*. New York: R. Martin, 1850.

Spira, S. F. "Graves and Graven Images." *History of Photography* 5, 4 (October 1981): 325–28.

Strangstad, Lynette. *A Graveyard Preservation Primer*. Nashville, Tenn.: American Association for State and Local History, 1988.

Tashjian, Dickran and Ann. *Memorials for Children of Change: The Art of Early New England Stonecarving*. Middletown, Conn.: Wesleyan University Press, 1974.

Vovelle, Michael. "A Century and One-Half of American Epitaphs (1660–1813): Toward the Study of Collective Attitudes about Death." *Comparative Studies in Society and History* 22, 4 (1980): 534–47.

The WPA Guide to 1930s New Jersey. New Brunswick: Rutgers University Press, 1986.

Wacker, Peter. *Land and People: A Cultural Geography of Preindustrial New Jersey*. New Brunswick: Rutgers University Press, 1975.

Wallis, Charles L. *Stories on Stone: A Book for American Epitaphs*. New York: Oxford University Press, 1954.

Wallis, Charles L. *American Epitaphs: Grave and Humorous*. New York: Dover Publications, 1973.

Wasserman, Emily. *Gravestone Designs, Rubbings and Photographs from Early New York and New Jersey.* New York: Dover Publications, 1972.

Welch, Richard F. *Memento Mori: The Gravestones of Early Long Island, 1680–1810.* Syosett, N.Y.: Friends for Long Island Heritage, 1983.

Welch, Richard F. "The New York and New Jersey Gravestone Carving Tradition." *Markers* 4 (1987): 1–54.

Westergaard, Barbara. *A Guide to the State.* New Brunswick: Rutgers University Press, 1981.

Wheeler, William Ogden, and Halsey, Edmund D. *Inscriptions on Tombstones: Elizabeth, New Jersey.* New Haven, Conn.: Tuttle, Morehouse and Taylor, 1892.

Wolfe, Laurance. "Stereotombs." *Stereo World,* January/February 1987, 5–14.

Wolk, Ruth. *The History of Woodbridge.* Woodbridge, N.J.: Woodbridge Publishing Co., 1957.

Genealogical Index

General Index

(Page numbers of main entries for burial grounds are in boldface.)

CPSIA information can be obtained at www.ICGtesting.com
Printed in the USA
BVOW041909221211

279042BV00003B/80/A